Twayne's English Authors Series

Sylvia E. Bowman, *Editor*

INDIANA UNIVERSITY

Laurence Sterne

(TEAS) 26

Laurence Sterne

By WILLIAM BOWMAN PIPER

Western Reserve University

Twayne Publishers, Inc.   ::   New York

To my father
Lewis A. Piper

Preface

The life of Laurence Sterne has been comprehensively described.[1] One can choose among numerous recent accounts of it for a sympathetic rendering, or among numerous nineteenth-century accounts for an unsympathetic one. The many biographies of Sterne also vary in length, with Wilbur Cross's monumental *Life and Times* at one extreme, Peter Quennell's neat "Laurence Sterne" at the other, and Lodwick Hartley's *This is Lorence* in between; and one can find a few pages in almost every edition of *Tristram Shandy* given over to the author's life. The wealth of biographies varies, yet again, in emphasis, different ones focussing individually on different aspects of Sterne's nature and career. One can read Margaret R. B. Shaw's *Laurence Sterne,* for instance, to learn about the origins of his humor and L. P. Curtis's *Sterne's Politics* to find out about his political activities.

One can, in short, discover from biographies of almost every length and slant such vital facts as these: Laurence Sterne (born 1713) was an obscure parson in the north of England who achieved literary fame almost overnight and rather late in life; his father, "a little smart man"[2] and a soldier, was mortally hurt in a duel over a goose; his widowed mother and his sister teased him into a scandalous squabble over money; he humored his wife in her delusion that she was the queen of Bohemia; he eased the tedium of his daily round by meeting with a group of self-styled demoniacs at a place they called Crazy Castle; he read widely in such authors as Rabelais, Montaigne, Cervantes, Burton, Locke, and Swift and copied from them in his own writings; he engaged in several flirtations after his marriage, the most serious of which came in his life's last flickering year; he suffered from consumption most of his life and may have contracted syphilis sometime along the way; he fenced against his infirmities with mirth, loved polite society, and died (1768) at his Bond Street lodgings in London. The amount of light such vital facts cast on Sterne's literary compositions may be questioned; but it is certain that the facts have been capably and extensively published.

The one fact of importance for the purposes of this study, *Laurence Sterne,* is that Laurence Sterne composed two literary masterpieces, *The Life and Opinions of Tristram Shandy, Gentleman* and *A Sentimental Journey Through France and Italy. Laurence Sterne* is, therefore, primarily a study of these two masterpieces. I take them up one at a time, *Tristram Shandy* in chapters 2-6 and *A Sentimental Journey* in chapters 8 and 9, and I describe as precisely as possible the form, the development, and the quality of each. To put this another way, in writing *Laurence Sterne* I have tried to follow Pope's famous dictum and read each of the two major effusions of Sterne's wit with the same spirit that its author writ.

My first major problem in making this study was to define the artistic stance of each work; that is, the social confrontation in *Tristram Shandy* and the empirical form of persuasion in *A Sentimental Journey.* These foundations of Sterne's two great novels, to which eighteenth-century minds must have been perfectly susceptible, are still accessible and, indeed, central to human consciousness today. But to recapture their freshness, to recognize their literary potentialities, modern readers need a little prompting, a few reminders, which this book attempts to furnish. Once we feel the dynamics of polite conversation as the eighteenth century felt it and as Sterne has recreated it for us and for all times in *Tristram Shandy,* we will see the volumes and the chapters of that apparently whimsical and unnatural novel emerge with almost the same inner necessity as that with which the branches and leaves emerge from a tree. And once we catch the drift of Yorick's empirically suggestive collection of sentimental experiences, the nature and validity of his teaching will virtually speak for themselves.

My second major problem in making this study was to curb my analysis of the two works at those points where objective description became subjective response. This interpretive restraint was especially hard and especially important to maintain in the presence of *Tristram Shandy,* which Sterne has focussed so sharply on the individual consciousness of his readers. To understand this novel in its total dimension one must keep reminding himself that every reader will, by Sterne's design, bring half the entertainment along with him—and that every reader will bring along something different. Many passages in *Tristram* have been designed by Sterne to give play to more than one response. Uncle Toby's amours, for instance, obviously makes an extensive comic appeal; but I have always found in the failure of this love, which should have joined in matrimony the pair most perfectly composed of all men and women to take on its duties and comforts, something tragic, a defeat for humanity and all human hopes; and there are, no doubt, other readers who find the story just a bit of bawdry.

Tristram's whole discourse, with its pauses and dodges and polite obliquities, allows the same variety of understandings. It was because nineteenth-century critics failed to curb or, indeed, even to recognize the subjectivity of their responses that their discussions of *Tristram* are so unsatisfactory, revealing not the novel but themselves. And many twentieth-century critics, who have crammed their minds with Freud and Proust and Joyce, while seeing the mistaken prudery of the Victorians, make essentially the same mistake. Both groups have looked into Sterne's magic mirror and seen only themselves. I have tried, on the other hand, to work invisibly and to observe Sterne's obvious intention that each reader should suffer and recognize his own responses or, as Tristram puts it, that the reader shall decide. My task in describing *Tristram Shandy*, then, has been to define the grounds and to highlight the elements of individual decision and to stop there.

The case of *A Sentimental Journey*, whose purpose, as described by both Yorick and Sterne, was to teach us to love mankind better than we do, is rather different. Beneath the provocative ambiguities of Yorick's sentimental instances lies an unambiguous teaching—or so it has seemed to me. And I have come to believe that this teaching lies at the heart of this brief novel just as the stress of individual decision lies at the heart of the longer and more complex *Tristram*. This work presents its choices of response and decision too, however; and I have tried to observe them.

The task I have set about, then, is the dusting and the polishing of Laurence Sterne's two great literary achievements. My aim is to bring out again the brilliance and the grace with which they impressed and captivated their own time. Their patina, like that of all great literary achievements, is actually the blindness and the prejudice of their readers. My job has been simply to adjust modern vision so that *Tristram Shandy* and *A Sentimental Journey* can stand forth in their own proper symmetry and luster.

References to other writings of Sterne, especially to his letters and sermons, occur incidentally in this study. But these works do not seem to warrant individual attention. The letters are, after all, sub-literary, hardly the proper objects together or separately for literary analysis; and the sermons belong to an outmoded form of literature and to a form, moreover, which depends for its primary effect on an oral delivery we cannot recapture. *A Political Romance*, Sterne's first real experiment in literature, is too rooted in York politics, practices, and personalities to claim any except the scholar's attention. Of course, these writings, like nearly everything Sterne touched, have the sparkle to gratify Sterne enthusiasts. But it is on *Tristram Shandy* and *A Sentimental Journey*, the two works which have pleased many and pleased long, that our attention must center.

In preparing *Laurence Sterne* I have drawn on the great wealth of Sterne scholarship, which I recognize throughout the book as pointedly as possible. I have also incurred many personal debts, the most obvious of which I wish herewith to acknowledge: first, to Professor Robert Greenberg, Professor Christopher Drummond, Professor William Ekstrom and, especially, Professor Ricardo Quintana for valuable advice and encouragement; second, to the editors of *Criticism* and *Studies in English Literature* for permission to re-use material which first appeared in those magazines; third, to the University of Louisville and Western Reserve University for financial assistance in completing and preparing my manuscript; fourth, to Professor Sylvia Bowman, the editor of the Twayne English Authors Series, for many suggestions and corrections; and, finally, to Katharine Welles Piper for many necessary acts of assistance and comfort.

WILLIAM BOWMAN PIPER

Western Reserve University

Contents

Contents

Chronology

1711   September 25, Laurence Sterne's parents, Roger Sterne, an ensign in the Thirty-fourth Regiment of Foot, and Agnes Nuttal Hebert, a captain's widow and a sutler's stepdaughter, are married.

1713   November 24, Laurence Sterne is born in Clonmel, Ireland, his parents' first son and second child.

1723   about. Put in a school near Halifax after a childhood spent following his father from one military post to another.

1731   His father dies in Jamaica.

1733   Enrolls at Jesus College, Cambridge, with which his family has had prior connections.

1737   Receives his B.A. degree; the M.A. follows in 1740.

1737   Appointed curate of St. Ives.

1738   Appointed to the living at Sutton-in-the-Forest.

1740-   Installed as prebendary for Givendale.
1741

1741   Marries Elizabeth Lumley and settles at Sutton-in-the-Forest; farms to augment his income (until 1758 when losses prompt him to give it up).

1741   Installed as prebendary for North Newbald—a reward for his political writing during the 1741 by-election.

1744   Appointed to the living at Stillington, near Sutton.

1747   His sermon, "The Case of Elijah and the widow of Zaraphath Considered," which he preached in York, is published there as a sixpenny pamphlet.

1747   December 1, Lydia Sterne, his only child to live long, is born.

1750   His sermon, "The Abuses of Conscience," which he preached in York, is published there as a sixpenny pamphlet.

1747- Suffers from a tangle of family problems; breaks with his
1751   uncle, the prosperous churchman Jacques Sterne; falls into
       a misunderstanding with his mother and his sister Cather-
       ine; charged, largely due to the machinations of his uncle,
       with neglecting his mother and sister.

1759   January, his satire, *A Political Romance* (since renamed
       The History of a Good Warm Watch-Coat), the climax
       of several years of experience with church politics, is pub-
       lished in York and, at the pleas of both friends and foes,
       quickly withdrawn.

1760   January 1, Volumes I and II of *Tristram Shandy* are pub-
       lished in London, a few copies having been released just
       previously in York.

1760   March, makes the first of several triumphal visits to Lon-
       don; sees his books through the press and enjoys their
       public reception.

1760   March, appointed to the living at Coxwold—moving there
       soon after his return north from London.

1760   April, the second edition of Volumes I and II of *Tristram*
       appears, augmented by Hogarth's frontispiece (of Trim
       reading the sermon) and by the tribute to Pitt.

1760   May, Volumes I and II of *The Sermons of Mr. Yorick,* with
       an apologetical preface and with Sterne's name on a second
       title page, are published in London.

1761   January 28, Volumes III and IV of *Tristram* are published
       in London.

1761   December 21, Volumes V and VI of *Tristram* are published
       in London (by T. Becket and P. A. Dehondt, who will
       henceforth replace R. and J. Dodsley as Sterne's pub-
       lishers).

1762   January, goes to France for his health after a severe hem-
       orrhage—one of many that plagued him from his college
       days to his death.

1762   February, reported dead, and widely eulogized.

1762   January-June, flatteringly received in Paris where he meets
       Diderot and other French intellectuals.

1762   July, Mrs. Sterne and Lydia follow him to Paris.

1762- Autumn-Spring, family lives at Toulouse in the south of
1763   France; Sterne often ill.

1763- Winter, family stops in Montpelier after a summer of
1764   travel; Sterne ill much of the time.

1764   June, returns to York, leaving Mrs. Sterne and Lydia in
       France.

1764   November, Volume VIII of *Tristram* (barely begun at
       Toulouse) is finished; he fits some material from his recent
       travels into the novel as Volume VII and thus makes up
       his usual two-volume installment.

1765   January, Volumes VII and VIII of *Tristram* are published
       in London.

1765- October-June, visits Europe again, this time staying chiefly
1766   in Italy.

1766   January, Volumes III and IV of *The Sermons of Mr. Yorick*
       are published in London (volumes V, VI, and VII to be
       brought out by Lydia after his death).

1766   June, returns to Coxwold; leaves Mrs. Sterne and Lydia
       in France.

1767   January, Volume IX of *Tristram* is published in London.

1767   January, meets Eliza Draper in London; enjoys an intense
       sentimental attachment with her.

1767   April, Eliza sails for India never to see him again.

1767   April, Sterne returns to Coxwold where (from April to
       November) the *Journal to Eliza* (first published in the
       1904 edition of the *Life and Works of Laurence Sterne*,
       edited by Wilbur Cross) accumulates.

1767- May-February, composes Volumes I and II of *A Senti-*
1768   *mental Journey.*

1767   September 30-November 1, Mrs. Sterne and Lydia visit him
       in Coxwold.

1768   February, Volumes I and II of *A Sentimental Journey* are
       published in London (with the promise of two more vol-
       umes).

1768   March 18, Sterne dies at his Bond Street lodging in London.

Laurence Sterne

CHAPTER 1

Introduction

LAURENCE STERNE'S *Tristram Shandy* and *A Sentimental Journey* are eighteenth-century English novels. This does not mean that they are outmoded like powdered wigs or minuets or feelings of condescension toward the American Colonies but, rather, that their enduring literary qualities are similar to those we find in the works of Swift, Fielding, and Johnson. Nor does it mean that we must know all about eighteenth-century English life and thought to understand them, although such knowledge illuminates some of their darker corners. But it does mean that we must clear our minds of nineteenth- and twentieth-century literary ideals and expectations. If we want to understand Sterne's two great novels themselves, we must not think of them as precursors to Thackeray or Dickens, to Proust or Joyce or Virginia Woolf. Instead we must read them afresh as Sterne's enthralled contemporaries did—trying, of course, to be the wise contemporaries Sterne wished for.

Tristram Shandy and *A Sentimental Journey* are typical eighteenth-century works, first, in their being told by self-conscious narrators who are publicly, socially oriented.[1] Tristram and Yorick face polite society just as Mr. Spectator, Lemuel Gulliver, and Mr. Rambler do; and they feel the same need to regulate their discourse so that they may provide society with entertainment and instruction. Many of the public narrators in eighteenth-century prose works are didactic and satiric ploys, masks rather than characters. Addison used Mr. Spectator, for instance, to get the detachment and anonymity his teachings required; and Swift used the Grub Street hack in *A Tale of a Tub* to sharpen and enrich his attack on pedantry and on arrogant ignorance. Sterne has, likewise, used Tristram and Yorick for his satiric purposes, variously employing them to attack pedantry, prudery, false gravity, and crabbed selfishness. But Tristram and Yorick also share in a second use that eighteenth-century literature often found for its public narrators, that of novelistic characters. Like Moll Flanders and Roderick Random, Tristram and Yorick suffer a complex of human feelings and entanglements and are thus capable of attracting human sympathy: Tristram tells society the story of his and his family's unfortunate life; Yorick shares with the public his sentimental French encounters.

A further way in which Sterne's novels are in keeping with their time is their wonderfully conversational style—one proper, of course, to their narrators' public, social orientations. The eighteenth century was the great age of English conversation. In this age John Wilkes was able to talk away his hideous face in half an hour, and Samuel Johnson, by the sheer brilliance of his address, could make the most elegant London companies endure his uncleanliness, his twitches, and his general bearishness. The age's conversational brilliance permeated its prose; indeed, James Sutherland describes eighteenth-century English prose as "a development from the conversation of English gentlemen." [2] Sutherland has referred to Addison and Swift as his examples, but Sterne's style is, if anything, more conversational than theirs. Sterne's chief stylistic intention, according to Wilbur Cross, was "to present the illusion of his natural speech with all its easy flow, warmth, and color." [3] That he achieved this intention we have the testimony of many of his readers. Virginia Woolf, for instance, has written that Sterne's sentences seem to "fall from the lips of a brilliant talker." [4]

Sterne's two novels, then, share with each other and with much other eighteenth-century English prose two important formal elements, the publicly oriented narrator and the conversational style. Sterne has employed these common eighteenth-century devices, however, in two crucially different ways.

Tristram Shandy, gentleman, the narrator of Sterne's first novel, is held continuously before a microcosmic, mixed-company audience, a society of ladies and gentlemen, who attend the unfolding of Tristram's discourse with unsteady interest and with varying degrees of approval; they even interrupt Tristram when he bores, disturbs, or confuses them. Tristram must constantly concern himself with their interest and understanding, and, because of this, his fluid communication is fraught with problems and perils: he may at any moment lose their attention by dwelling on a Shandy peculiarity or offend their sensibilities with an item of Shandy privacy. This is especially true since the life story he must tell is in large part tediously peculiar and hopelessly obscene. Parson Yorick, the narrator of *A Sentimental Journey,* on the other hand, has been set in the comfort of his study to compose, for later publication, a report of his recent French experiences and to teach the lesson of sentiment's social efficacy which they exemplify. Yorick is vividly aware of his audience—but only as readers, never as restless and interrupting guests. His material is also much easier to publicize than Tristram's was since it is not private and personal but public and social.

Each of Sterne's narrators discourses in the style which his own situation and his own narrative material require. Tristram is the giddy and flexible entertainer, always dynamically involved with his audience and his material, in danger every moment of losing the sympathy of the one and his control over the other, constantly striving to find a method for making each odd item of his life a source of general entertainment and instruction. Yorick is the confident clergyman who takes advantage of his leisure to arrange, polish, and judge his recent social activities and pleasures and to insinuate their general social significance. The style of each narrator has been nicely suggested by Alice Green Fredman, who describes Tristram's as "an unpredictable flow of life" and Yorick's as one of "exquisite precision." [5]

Our study of both novels will be concerned with the narrator's efforts to make his personal experiences effectively public. But, as this brief comparison suggests, we will find their problems and their solutions strikingly different. To make this study and to define the literary effects Sterne has derived from each of his employments of the publicly oriented narrator, we will naturally have to consider his two novels separately. Our chief goal will be to describe as precisely as possible the special qualities first of one and then of the other.

This study of *Tristram Shandy* and *A Sentimental Journey,* however, will naturally bring out many other general elements, besides their use of the public narrator and their conversational style, which they share with their century. We will notice, for instance, that Sterne is much closer to John Locke ideologically than he would have been had he made "the association of ideas" the cement for Tristram's or Yorick's discourse.[6] We will notice, again, that time, which the moderns have found subjectively pliable, is for Sterne as for Locke essentially stiff, recalcitrant, unmanageable—one of the inevitable limitations to human hopes and actions.[7] Indeed, Sterne will generally emerge as another great eighteenth-century spokesman of man's limitations and fraility, as one who clearly perceives what Arnold Kettle has called "the cussedness of life." [8] This study will also reveal, differently but powerfully in each novel, that empirical feeling for the relationship between particular experience and general truth which moved strongly not only in Locke and Hume but also in Fielding and Johnson. We should come to see, finally, that *Tristram Shandy* and *A Sentimental Journey* share with other literary works of their time a quality of poise and order much greater at least than most modern readers have been prepared or able to recognize. Both works are loose, in somewhat the same way that Pope's *Epistle to Dr. Arbuthnot* and that Johnson's *Rasselas* are loose; but they also share something of the balance, the sense of discrimination and limitation, and the same high polish that those works have.

PART I

Tristram Shandy

CHAPTER 2

Tristram's Dilemma

LAURENCE STERNE has placed the narrator-hero of his *The Life and Opinions of Tristram Shandy, Gentleman*[1] in a dilemma: he has, on the one hand, continuously held Tristram in social conversation and, on the other, made him describe a life whose vital facts are unfit for social utterance. Sterne has given his novel its form and its central meanings by exploiting this dilemma. To define it, we must understand its conflicting components—Tristram's social situation; and the socially unmentionable facts of his life.

I *Tristram's Social Situation*

Tristram has hopes of raising himself and, like any dutiful heir, of exalting his family; but his chances for normal achievement, as he will report (41;166;230), were flattened long ago. However, by making his discourse socially affecting, he can still win some eminence for himself and all the Shandys. He has thus explicitly dedicated his story's choicest morsel, Uncle Toby's amours (337;466), and its chief formal principle, his mingling of life and opinions (10-11), to society's entertainment and edification. If he can tell his life story entertainingly and make it widely appealing, Tristram may hope that it will remain as a lasting treasure for the curious (66); that it will "swim down the gutter of Time" along with *A Tale of a Tub* (610); that it will become, like Montaigne's *Essays* and Bunyan's *Pilgrim's Progress,* "a book for the parlour-window" (7).

Tristram solicits society's attention on almost every page, often making general addresses to "my good people" or "readers" and often speaking more selectively to "Madam," "Sir," "My Dear Girl," and "Your Worships and Reverences." His addresses to them are various: he prays for their attention (188;577) or their

reliance on his powers (11;613); he assures them of his sincerity
(457) and of his concern for them (286;403-4); he kisses their
hands (84). He has teased them (11;337), scolded them (56-57;
602), and enticed them with promises (337;363). His desire for
their close involvement in his story has even led him to leave
them spaces in his discourse—spaces for them to criticize him
(84), for them to draw their own ideas of Widow Wadman
(470-71), for them to curse (529), and, above all, spaces for them
to fill with their own imaginations(108-9;218). And Tristram has
been careful to tell his audience that these spaces have been left
especially for them. Thackeray's complaint about Tristram (although he was attacking Tristram's creator) that "this man . . .
never lets his reader alone, or will permit his audience repose"[2]
correctly reflects the constancy if not the tone of Tristram's social solicitation.

The individual occasions for these social attentions are not all
obscene, as Thackeray and other Victorians seem to have felt. Of
course, many are. Often, when Tristram verges on indecency, he
shows great regard for Madam's imagination, warning her to
read on rapidly (75-76) or to guard her fancies (226;367-68;602).
At other times he just drops what may seem like bawdy hints and
passes on (185-86;215;551). However, Tristram also calls on his
audience when he is opening a difficult or peculiar element of his
story (188;63;154;455-56)—especially when he must suspend it
to explain it or fill in its background (7-8;351;382;434). Once or
twice he has even asked his audience for narrative advice (207)
or assistance (455;285-87). Tristram solicits attention directly,
again, when his story has led him to one of his opinions. Opinions
on home and family (56;114;434) he usually addresses to
Madam, those on literature and philosophy (5;85;185-86; 192-203;
313-16;373) to Sir, and those on conduct (15-17;162;164ff;292-94)
to them both.

Tristram's concern for the interest and approval of society goes
further still: he suffers its members to interrupt him. Madam cuts
in on some of his seemingly bawdy talk, sometimes with reproof
(49) and sometimes with curiosity (272;625). Both Madam and
Sir have interrupted Tristram when they could not follow his
story (226) or when they were excited about its development
(115). They sometimes complain that the relevance of an epi-

sode or an opinion escapes them (5;56;511). Tristram usually responds to these interruptions with great circumspection; he defends himself from Madam's reproof (49); he tries to translate the tale from Slawkenbergius that will assuage her curiosity about the truth of Diego's nose (272-73); he helps Sir understand his unlucky conception by giving him a little lesson on the homunculus (5-6); and he greets Sir's question about the identity of Tickletoby's mare with the exhortation to Sir to "Read, read, read, read" (226). Tristram is so sensitive to his audience, indeed, that he usually anticipates their interruptions. Here, for instance, he has forestalled Madam's prudery: "My uncle *Toby's* opinion, Madam, 'that there could be no harm in *Cornelius Gallus*, the *Roman* prætor's lying with his wife;'—or rather the last word of that opinion,—(for it was all my mother heard of it) caught hold of her by the weak part of the whole sex:—You shall not mistake me,—I mean her curiosity" (367-68). One can almost see Madam raise—and then lower—her eyebrows. Tristram is equally sensitive to society's curiosity (377;602), to the limits of its learning (85;225;395-97), and to its need for narrative background and explanation (154;207).

Sterne has heightened this impression of his narrator's deep and continuous social involvement by giving him a style widely recognized as conversational. An obvious sign of this is Tristram's use of such words as "say," "speak," "mention," "tell," and "talk" to describe his discourse. Tristram concludes an early utterance of his defiance of critics, "I need not tell your worship, all this is spoke in confidence" (36). Another way Sterne makes Tristram seem like a conversationalist is by pushing him headlong through his story: Tristram is unable to go back and revise (462-63;515-16); he is unsure whether he has already told something or not (479); and he is unwilling to blot (511). Time hurries Tristram, as it would naturally hurry a talker (and not a writer): sometimes things crowd in on him so thick and threefold that he does not know which to tell first, and he feels strongly that he may never get to everything (235;280;336-37). He is sometimes too rushed to verify his sources and references (24;63;350-51). He finds that the time he has set aside for a digression (618) and, indeed, for his whole book (285-86; 397;610-11) is slipping away from him. The shifting of Tristram's notions too, especially that shift between admissions of literary helplessness and claims of consummate control, adds to the impression of Tristram as a conversationalist, as an entertaining talker, who catches many of his narrative and opinionative opportunities but not all of them.

Tristram actually thinks of his style as a form both of talking and writing; and we can often catch him shifting between the two, as in this passage:

All my heroes are off my hands;—'tis the first time I have had a moment to spare,—and I'll make use of it, and write my preface.

THE
AUTHOR's PREFACE.
No, I'll not say a word about it,—here it is;—in publishing it,—I have appealed to the world,—and to the world I leave it;—it must speak for itself.   (192)

He clearly thinks of the Preface, a formal item, as written (although it must "speak for itself"); but the introductory, transitional material is pure talk. He also shifts between writing and talking in putting his dedicatory epistle up for sale (14-15) and, again, in this passage: "Here,—but why here,—rather than in any other part of my story,—I am not able to tell;—but here it is, —my heart stops me to pay to thee, my dear uncle *Toby*, once for all, the tribute I owe thy goodness. Here let me thrust my chair aside, and kneel down upon the ground, whilst I am pouring forth the warmest sentiments of love for thee, and veneration for the excellency of thy character, that ever virtue and nature kindled in a nephew's bosom" (224). Tristram has been seated at his desk writing; but this sudden swell of emotion requires a relief which only speech can give. This mixture of writing and talking comes naturally to Tristram, for to him "writing, when properly managed, (as you may be sure I think mine is) is but a different name for conversation" (108-10).

The shiftiness of this writing-talking style, its gaps, detours, and digressions, Tristram has explicitly laid to his social situation and intentions (10-11;72-74;108-10). True, its wonderful responsiveness to each moment's vibrations does occasionally, as in his prayer to Uncle Toby (90), reflect Tristram's inner feelings—but not very often. Generally, as we will see, it changes course, admits a digression, or leaves a gap as a result of Tristram's concern for his audience. Wayne Booth would suggest, indeed, that its course and form are completely determined by Tristram's social situation and by his social consciousness.[3]

But Tristram's social solicitation alone would not have made his discourse the involved, digressive, circuitous thing it is. Indeed, Tristram feels that he must apologize to society at the end of Volume VI for his narrative vagaries, and he promises that he will tell his story more directly hereafter (473-75). It is actually the social unsuitableness of the private Shandy history which he is trying to make public that has forced Tristram to suspend and tangle his discourse, that has made him digress, double back, and leave gaps. To understand this history's social unsuitableness, however, we must first understand its basic facts and nature.

II *The Facts of Tristram's Life*

The facts, which I have abstracted from Tristram's whole discourse elsewhere,[4] are really quite simple. Tristram Shandy, gentleman, has begun towards the end of his life to address society, which he calls the world, telling it about those early misfortunes by which his odd character and his narrow destiny were determined. That those misfortunes have rendered him sexually impotent is pervasively suggested, as James A. Work has noticed,[5] but never explicitly certified. What does become certain, as Tristram's discourse accumulates without his ever addressing or even mentioning any younger Shandys, is that he is childless. Tristram does refer to some sort of personal relationship with his dear Jenny (48-49;517-18). But regardless of its nature, it is clear by the novel's last volume (610-11) that she is growing old with Tristram and that there is no little Toby nor innocent Dinah to rival her in his affections. Since Tristram's brother Bobby died young (336ff) and since Uncle Toby Shandy died celibate (101), Tristram's childlessness means the extinction of the curious family whose memorialist and whose last survivor he is. Tristram's often admitted consumption, especially as it has been dramatized by his flight from death, assures us, furthermore, that Tristram's death and his family's extinction are very near. The cessation of his writing, indeed, with a one volume installment which neatly wraps up all of Tristram's discursive promises,[6] we may take as the signal of his demise, especially since Tristram has often equated his writing with his life (37;73-74;162;286;479). Tristram's social communication, then, is essentially a pitiful and a dreary one: in describing his decisively unlucky beginnings and in revealing his hopelessly dwindling age, he has been telling the world about his whole family's decline and fall.

The few pieces of narrative material out of which Tristram has fashioned his communication all focus sharply upon this personal and familial desolation. Telling the world about his conception (4-9), his birth (9-277), his naming (277-331), and his mutilation (372-442) has allowed Tristram to account for his lifelong misfortunes and to suggest powerfully their family significance. His telling of Bobby's early death (331-372) and of Toby's choice of celibacy (443-647) has made it clear that with his lonely death the family ends. Thus every major episode of family history taken up by Tristram has helped him bring out the central point of his communication: in himself his beloved family is dying out.

Not only has every episode in his story helped Tristram to assert his and his family's doom; each one also allows him, with his circumstantial manner of narration, to make a full display of the Shandy people and the Shandy qualities that the world is soon to lose. These few episodes allow Tristram, as D. W. Jefferson recognized,[7] to tell everything about his life and his family that he had to tell. The detailed report of a dozen or so days of Shandy life, as seen in the mirror of his detached but loving regard, accounts for all. We have a vivid sense of Tristram himself, at least as a public figure; wonderfully rounded descriptions of those Shandys and Shandy acquaintances who determined his life and dwell in his heart; and even a sense of the glimmering Shandy past with its glories, its shames, and its long decline. Tristram has not given the world a Shandy chronicle; but his peculiarly selective and expansive way with his Shandy material reflects this last Shandy's sense of his family, his own deep family involvement, and their common destiny more richly and pointedly than any conventional year-by-year report could have done.

The form of Tristram's Shandy history and its formal breaks are also remarkably useful in bringing out the vital facts of his communication. Formally Tristram's self-presentation is a two-ply affair: himself, as an adult, speaking to society in the present time;

himself, as an infant, described in the throes of private long-ago misfortunes. This extensive double presence of the hero (4-443) underscores his family involvement and the powerful causal relationship, often explicitly stated, between what happened to him long ago and what he is and what he is suffering now. The two interruptions to this two-ply form of self-portraiture —Uncle Toby's amours (443-647) and Tristram's present-day flight from death (479-538)—also have narrative significance. Tristram's turning so self-consciously from his early misadventures to Uncle Toby's amours (443) strongly suggests that Tristram has told us all about his own life that he needs to tell us. Early in the story he may have planned (36;74)—Sterne may have planned—[8] to fill in some of his life between the ages of five and forty; but now Tristram is telling us, simply by deserting his early life so completely after its fifth year, that he has told us enough. Those thirty-five unreported years, with all their whips, short turns, and vexations, contained nothing of importance that cannot be inferred from the major catastrophes of his infancy or filled in in passing as he focusses on Uncle Toby.

Tristram's abrupt interruption of Uncle Toby's amours with his own recent flight from death (479-538) has a different narrative value: it should make us understand how near the gaunt jester is to his life's end and how the pressures of time and disease are working on his discourse. The flight casts over the resumed telling of Toby's amours—a narrative which crystallizes with tremendous speed once Tristram has arranged the necessary data before us— a shadow of urgency and finality. With this, his choicest morsel— if he can get it told—Tristram will have satisfactorily completed his roles as Shandy historian and as social entertainer.

Tristram's artful selection of his episodes, then, and his two-ply presentation of himself help him to focus and to emphasize the key facts of his life story. But virtually all of these vitally significant episodes, especially in the detailed and circumstantial accounts which Tristram has given them, are profoundly unsuitable to social communication. We must understand just how, and just how deeply unsuitable they are to understand the problem Tristram faces in giving them social utterance.

III *The Social Unsuitableness of the Facts*

They are socially unsuitable, first, because of their tremendous peculiarity and oddity.[9] None of the vital family events that Tristram has reported seems, at least at first glance, to resemble anything that could trouble a normal member of society: thus none of them seems likely to awaken any social sympathy or attention. Walter's concern over his son's nose and name, for instance, and the peculiarly appropriate defeats he suffers are hardly calculated to strike a sympathetic chord in Madam or in Sir. Nor are any of Walter's or Toby's efforts on behalf of the public likely to stir general gratitude or admiration. Walter thought of himself as a metaphysical pioneer, truly; Toby believed that he was advancing England's destiny in his bowling-green campaigns; and the dutiful Tristram has tried to make something of these public benefactions, giving the title of the "Shandean System," for instance, to his father's notion of names (68). But most of society will be inclined to find Walter's great philosophical speculations too odd to take seriously; and their patriotism will hardly be fired by Toby's military activities. Madam and Sir will probably find even the physical objects that figured in Shandy history—such things as a library of noses, a parlor door's squeaky hinge, a few lead weights, some old military maps, and two Turkish pipes—too peculiar to draw their attention. But since these interests, actions, and objects are vital to Shandy destiny and typical of Shandy life, Tristram must give them whatever social currency he can. First of all, he must explain their relevance to his life, showing under what train of circumstances such things as a set of hard knots, a cut thumb, and a loose forceps came to figure in it. Second, and more important, he must give these odd interests, actions, and objects some kind of general value. He must make Madam and Sir see in one odd element of his story after another some lesson or opinion, some warning or application, or, at least, some joke in which they can find edification or entertainment.

The crucial episodes of Tristram's life are socially unsuitable, in the second place, because they are so pitiful and painful. Every episode reveals a Shandy loss: Tristram is misbegotten; he is damaged in birth; he is given exactly the wrong name; his brother dies; he is mutilated in childhood; his Uncle Toby, despite being

[28]

perfectly formed to be a husband and a father, is driven to give up all ideas of marriage. The vital facts amount to an unbroken series of losses, each made up of smaller losses and all adding up to the complete loss of the family. We may think of this history as tragic or as merely dreary;[10] but it is obviously, in either case, the hardest kind of stuff to turn into social entertainment. How can Tristram give it the light tone, the gay accent? How can he transform it—not falsify it—so as to amuse an audience who, if he should grow tearful or become depressing, will desert him for cards, gossip, or more lively company?

A third and the most obvious aspect of Tristram's problem of public adjustment is his story's unavoidable obscenity. If a mere recollection of its subject matter—of such things as Tristram's conception and his Uncle Toby's wound—did not assure us of its obscenity, the Victorians would tell us about it. "There is not a page," writes Thackeray, "but has something that were better away, a latent corruption—a hint, as of an impure presence."[11] Walter Bagehot, again, describes *Tristram Shandy* as "incurably tainted with a pervading vice; it dwells at length on, it seeks after, it returns to, it gloats over, the most unattractive part of the world."[12] Tristram returns to his unattractive part, of course, because for him it has been a vital part. His problem, as these quotations from Thackeray and Bagehot should have made clear, is to give society as full and precise a description of the obscene but vital Shandy events as he can without crossing society's hazy but tyrannically defended line of decency. He must tell what he can, suggest what he cannot tell, and protect himself at all times.

Tristram has sometimes given explicit notice to these three general aspects of this great discursive problem of private-public adjustment. He recognizes his story's extreme peculiarity (7-8) and sees that it will demand more explanation from him than he really wants to give (206-07) and more patience (10-11) and much more attention (56-57) from the members of society than they commonly practice. He sees his story, again, as a tragicomedy (600), as a string of "little evils and distresses" (215), and himself as a small, suffering hero (10). His sense of his story's obscenity and of his audience's prudery, of course, permeates his discourse.

But Tristram is too attentive to the special discursive problems of each item in his unfolding story to categorize the whole problem as I have done. What Sterne has given us throughout Tristram's discourse is the impression of a highly developed social consciousness brilliantly and variously at work on recalcitrant but vividly felt autobiographical material. We cite, for example, Tristram's introduction to his father's concern over his given name:

I would sooner undertake to explain the hardest problem in Geometry, than pretend to account for it, that a gentleman of my father's great good sense,—knowing, as the reader must have observed him, and curious, too, in philosophy,—wise also in political reasoning,—and in polemical (as he will find) no way ignorant,—could be capable of entertaining a notion in his head, so out of the common track,—that I fear the reader, when I come to mention it to him, if he is the least of a cholerick temper, will immediately throw the book by; if mercurial, he will laugh most heartily at it;—and if he is of a grave and saturnine cast, he will, at first sight, absolutely condemn as fanciful and extravagant; and that was in respect to the choice and imposition of Christian names, on which he thought a great deal more depended than what superficial minds were capable of conceiving.   (49-50)

Almost every narrative item Tristram must take up is doubly or trebly unsuitable for social discourse, this business on names typically being both odd and, eventually, pitiful; and every item is unsuitable in its own way. Thus Tristram's methods of transforming them, of turning these variously peculiar, pitiful, and obscene facts of his life into sparkling, widely appealing conversation, are various—too various to be catalogued.[13]

Nevertheless, by following the three aspects of his discursive problem here suggested, we can discuss the problem and Tristram's solutions of it conveniently and comprehensively; and, in so doing, we can approach a definition of Sterne's total novelistic achievement. The ensuing three chapters on *Tristram Shandy*, then, will cover Tristram's social accommodation, first, of his life story's peculiarity; second, of its tragedy; and, third, of its obscenity.

CHAPTER 3

Tristram's Digressive Artistry

TRISTRAM SHANDY hopes, as he says to Sir, that "nothing which has touched me will be thought trifling in its nature, or tedious in its telling" (10-11). But he knows that the figures and events which have touched him decisively, although not really trifling, are yet peculiar enough to seem so: his father was possessed by "an infinitude of oddities" (382); his Uncle Toby was a man of "great singularity" (78); his whole family, indeed, was "of an original character throughout" (65). And the crucial events of his life, with their deep family involvement, are naturally peculiar too. Tristram must preserve this peculiarity of his life and of his family to preserve their truth; but, if he is to make them interesting and important to society, he must also make them generally understandable and generally significant.

That he has succeeded in doing so we have the valuable testimony of Samuel Taylor Coleridge, who wrote that Sterne had achieved in *Tristram Shandy* "the novelty of an individual peculiarity together with the interest of a something that belongs to our common nature." [1] He has observed, particularly, in Toby's freeing of the fly "how individual character may be given . . . humanity." In this case Coleridge seems to have laid the interpenetration of the peculiar and the general to "the mere delicacy of the presentation"; but elsewhere he has spoken more suggestively: he detected in Sterne, as in other great humorists, "a certain reference to the general and the universal" which Sterne had achieved by bringing "the finite great . . . into identity with the little, or the little with the finite great." Applying these terms particularly to *Tristram Shandy,* we may say that Tristram has brought "the little," which was his peculiar life, into variously significant relationships with "the finite great," which was his wide social audience. In this chapter we must try to see how he has done this, and how it has affected the quality of Sterne's novel.

It is chiefly through Tristram's two main kinds of digression, explanatory and opinionative, that Tristram makes his peculiar life generally clear and broadly interesting. With his explanatory digressions, he defines his story's connections and fills in its background so that society can follow its crucial events and understand their Shandy importance. With his opinionative digressions, he derives from these events the widely relevant wit and instruction that will hold society's interest and attention. To understand this use of the digressions, which Sterne's critics have variously misunderstood,[2] we must analyze, first, their external references and, second, their internal forms.

I *The Digressions' External References*

Tristram generally introduces his explanatory digressions, to begin with these, just where they are needed, starting some of them, such as his description of Toby's character (63), in the middle of story sentences. And he usually asserts their explanatory value right away, stating that they will explain, translate, or give reasons (158;217;319;434;520;624; etc.). We take, for instance, this introduction to an explanatory digression: "What was the cause of this movement, and why I took such long strides in uttering this—I might leave to the curious too; but as no principle of clock-work is concern'd in it—'twill be as well for the reader if I explain it myself" (520). Tristram uses here not only "explain" but also the logical term "cause": he will explain the cause of his long strides. Tristram commonly concludes his explanatory digressions with a similarly formal assertion of their relationship, as in his conclusion to the digression whose introduction has just been quoted: "In my list, therefore, of *Videnda* at *Lyons,* this [the tomb of the two lovers], tho' *last*—was not, you see, *least;* so taking a dozen or two of longer strides than usual across my room, just whilst it passed my brain, I walked down calmly into the *Basse Cour,* in order to sally forth" (522). "Therefore" here reflects "cause" in the introduction. Tristram has further defined the use and the extent of this digression by repeating the "long strides" which it has been explaining. He introduces his digression on Phutatorius's exclamation (319-22) also to "explain" the "cause"; and he concludes it by repeating that exclamation which was the "effect" of this cause. Although his terms are not always so philosophical as this, Tristram generally brackets his explanatory digressions with assertions of their value and with definitive repetition.

These digressions have, moreover, the explanatory values Tristram claims for them. Tristram explains his long strides "to the curious," for instance, as a sign of his great desire to walk out to the tomb of the two lovers. Trim's make-believe artillery, again, which Tristram set off to explain "as I generally do, at a little distance from the subject" (449-54), has been vividly, unforgettably realized by the time Tristram brings in Uncle Toby to direct its fire. Tristram likewise explains in detail Trim's feeling of guilt over the window-sash accident (377-78) which, as he said, his readers could never imagine on their own. And he presents the background and nature of Walter's two beds of justice in his digression on that subject (434-36) better, perhaps, than Madam, for whose sake he has taken the trouble, could wish. There are a few digressions, explanatory of Shandy life, whose actual explanatory connections are weak. The long digression filling his readers in on Toby's character (63-99), for instance, holds up nothing more characteristic of Toby than his suggestion to ring the bell; and that on Yorick (17-35) explains, as Tristram admits, very little of the action at Shandy Hall. But these early digressions are exceptions to Tristram's explanatory rule. Tristram generally introduces explanatory digressions where they are needed to explain to his audience just what he says they need to have explained.

He is sometimes tardy in telling his audience the exact narrative relevance of an explanatory digression. He has started on the digression about his father's concern for names (49-56), for instance, without making it clear to the reader how this information, which explains events his narrative has not yet reached, will apply. He has likewise introduced the digression on his father's weakness for his own eloquence (351-53) merely by asking Your Worships' leave "to squeeze in a story between these two pages." But Tristram makes the explanatory relevance of these digressions perfectly clear before he concludes them. In these cases, as in the others, Tristram has paused to explain the odd elements of his story, knowing full well that he "is obliged continually to be going backwards and forwards to keep all tight together in the reader's fancy" (462).

Tristram's opinionative digressions are introduced to generalize the odd events of his life, that is, to draw from these events lessons and applications of broadly human value, and thus to make them meaningful to his audience. Tristram takes his mother's insistence on the midwife, for instance, as an example of a common trait in human psychology (44). He finds evidence in Dr. Slop's rehearsal of Ernulphus's curse for the opinion that none of us invents his own curses (180). From his own tearing out of a chapter (313-16), again, and his struggle to raise his imaginative powers (614-18), Tristram derives generally applicable opinions on literary composition. Opinionative digressions follow immediately the narrative matter from which they derive; and their connections are always clear. Tristram's opinion of curses comes right after Dr. Slop's rendering of Ernulphus's curse (179-80); his opinion on the tearing out of chapters follows hard on the chapter (XXIV of Volume IV) which Tristram has just torn out (302-13). To be sure that we recognize this chapter's omission and, thus, the present relevance of his opinion, Tristram begins: "—No doubt, Sir—there is a whole chapter wanting here."

Tristram directs each of these opinionative digressions, by which he hopes to deepen his audience's sense of involvement in his life story (10-11), toward those people most likely to benefit from it. Trim's hat dropping, for instance, leads Tristram to an opinion beneficial to "Ye who govern this mighty world [etc.]" (362). He aims his opinion on the homunculus (5-6) at the gentlemen in his audience, his opinions on wishes (157) and feminine vanity (364) at the ladies, and his opinion on baptism at them both (56-62). He directs his opinion on the dangers to total literary effects of brilliant episodes, more pointedly, at Your Reverences (313), his opinion on the causes of mental confusion at Sir Critic (85), and his opinion on the dangers of the erotic imagination at My Dear Girl (226).

Many of Tristram's digressions have values for his audience both as explanation and opinion; they explain a Shandy event and suggest a lesson or example of general applicability. In Toby's peculiar kindness toward the fly (113-14), for example, which was introduced merely to illustrate Toby's remarkable goodness of heart, Tristram finds an example which will serve "parents and governors instead of a whole volume upon the subject." His account of Trim's oratorical stance (120-23), which he introduced merely to "give you a description of his attitude," Tristram concludes by addressing more sharply to artists and orators as a model for such attitudes. His explanation of Dr. Slop's✱✱✱✱✱✱ (185-86) allows Tristram to give Your Worships and Reverences, the usual recipients of such opinions, a point on the decline of oratory and, having done that, to illuminate for them a moment in the drama on his birthday at Shandy Hall.

There is one further type of digression, the interlude, which we must notice before concluding this part of our analysis. Tristram's digressive interludes do not explain events of Tristram's life; nor do they derive from it as his opinionative digressions do: they are, rather, separate items of public discourse. Accordingly, Tristram introduces them only at major breaks in his narrative—at the termini of volumes, as in the case of the Slawkenbergius (244-71) and Whiskers anecdotes (343-48), or at the natural breaks in his story, as in the case of the violin recital which punctuates what Tristram has called his life's first act (371-72). The interludes refer only to Tristram's audience, not to his story—as he perfectly understands. With some of them, such as the Preface (192-203) and the salutations at the ends of volumes, Tristram fulfills customary obligations; others, like the Chapters (281-83) and Whiskers interludes, he presents as special courtesies. The Whiskers anecdote, indeed, he has revealed, much against his will, only because he made the world a promise of it (337;343). Tristram has made the most of his interludes' social appeal: he flirts with his audience's prudery in the Green Gowns (363) and Whiskers interludes; carries his point with an *ad hominem* argument in the Preface; and puts his dedication (13-17) up for public sale.

We may now say that all of Tristram's digressions—all except for a very few transparent, emotional ones (90;166;244)—were introduced to attract and hold Tristram's audience. He has explained his story and derived opinions from it to make it clear to his audience and to give its odd items a generally didactic or edifying value. And he has so defined and presented his digressions that his audience should have no trouble in understanding the special relevance of every one to itself. We must now turn to the internal forms of Tristram's digressions to make sure that he has composed them simply and clearly enough for Madam, Sir, and others like them to follow.

II *The Digressions' Internal Forms*

Tristram's many short digressions, which perform such common narrative functions as asking for attention, filling in background, and voicing asides, are easy to follow. So are his long chronological digressions, such as the story of Lefever or the tale from Slawkenbergius. It is the long non-chronological, or partly chronological, digressions, which are the most peculiar to Tristram's art, that must be examined. We will find that virtually all of them fall into two or three clearly defined and related sections.

Digressions of two balanced, parallel sections are common. In one of these (144-54), for instance, Tristram has a point to remind his readers of and a point to inform them about. He is careful, not only in introducing this digression, but also in shifting from its first to its second point, to assert its two-part form. He likewise separates his digression on his troubles (545) into two parts: there is, first, his trouble as an author and, second, his trouble as a man. He sees, on another occasion (368-69), two ways by which Eleazer may have received from the East his opinion that none of us is born to be a slave: there is, first, the water way and, second, the land way. He develops several digressions by telling, first, what is not the case and, second, what is the case. He gives in one digression (85-87), for instance, what did not cause Toby's confusion and then what did cause it. And in another (543-45) he tells what causes of sexual attraction do not account for Mrs. Wadman's attraction to Toby and then, as he is able, what cause does account for it.

Most of these clear and simply formed digressions, despite their formal balance, move toward communicative climaxes, toward main points. That the negative-to-positive digressions should do so is obvious; but others also rise to their closes. What Tristram reminds his audience of, for instance, is merely his father's eccentricity in general; what he informs them about is that particular eccentricity, Walter's concern for the cerebella of emergent fœtuses, which his story is now coming to. Tristram's trouble as an author, again, is merely the slow sales of his book;

his trouble as a man is a recent great loss of blood. And Tristram concludes the two ways by which Eleazer may have got his opinion by exclaiming, no matter which way the opinion came, what a time of it the learned had in Eleazer's day. A most striking case of parallel construction and rhetorical climax is furnished by Tristram's argument for believing that his father did not write the chapter on window sashes in the *Tristrapædia* before his own window sash accident (383-84). Tristram gives two reasons: the first is that, had his father written the chapter before the accident, it would surely have been averted; the second is that he has written this chapter of his father's book himself. Thus Tristram can lead his audience through two balanced sections of digression in a pointed and emphatic fashion which his conversational ease may disguise but does not nullify.

The parts of Tristram's longer bipartite digressions are often more tightly related than this. Tristram is very fond, for instance, of the general statement and its exception. He will prove to everybody except a connoisseur, he says on one occasion (180-83), that we have not invented our own oaths. He starts with the exception, satirically obliterating all connoisseurs, and, having done that, he makes his proof to everybody else. The proof, by the way, is developed in two balancing sections: it is developed by the artistic argument, which Tristram himself professes, and by the scholarly argument, attributed to Walter. Tristram's digression on sleep (288-91) also contains a point, that bookish men can say nothing good on the subject, and then an exception, something pretty good from Montaigne. In the dedicatory chapter on hobby horses (13-15), Tristram has given the exception a graceful complimentary emphasis. No man's riding of his own hobby horse hurts anyone else *except* in the case of your Lordship (the prospective purchaser of the dedication) who may be neglecting the high callings of patriotism and glory.

Tristram's most difficult digressions, when subjected to analysis, will be seen to fall into structures of closely related parts. His curious explanation of his way with his life's little misfortunes (517-18), for instance, is made up of an ambiguously beasterisked anecdote which illustrates his way of "making a penny of every one of 'em'" and of an argument in which he takes literally this idea of making pennies and claims that he would make pounds out of "good cursed bouncing losses." Tristram concludes this digression by defining just the good bouncing loss, that is, just the financially valuable one, he desires: it is one worth "a hundred [pounds] a year or so." Tristram's argumentative Preface on wit and judgment (192-203) is also composed of two sections: there is a minor point—that wit and judgment are in somewhat short supply; and a major point—that each man has been endowed with just the amount of judgment that his amount of wit requires.[3] The late digression by which Tristram has recommended his way of raising his creative powers (614-18) contains not two but three main parts: the first, on poor methods for raising one's powers; the second, on Tristram's good method (shaving); the third, on objections to this method. Tristram has developed it by variously using almost every formal device we have uncovered: the parallel, the negative-to-positive, the illustration and the exception; and he works the whole wonderfully fluid passage into an almost Scholastic form of argument.

The digression introducing, first, Uncle Toby's minor traits and, second, his major ones (63-99) is probably the most difficult and involved in the novel. Indeed, its first part is briefly marred by a confusion. Tristram should have introduced Toby's and Walter's argument over Aunt Dinah into this first part merely as an illustration of Toby's minor traits of modesty and family pride. But he has actually presented this argument as a matter of the first communicative importance, to which the revelation of Toby's traits is ancillary. The story of the argument has come up at the mention of Aunt Dinah in the introductory paragraph on the family or blood origins of Toby's character, before any of Toby's minor traits has been mentioned. In the next two paragraphs Tristram dedicates himself solely to getting this story straight. Thus when Toby's modesty and family pride are finally discovered, they seem like mere background material to the story of the argument, both of them being required if the audience is to understand the argument. It is by following the argument over Aunt Dinah, moreover, that Tristram will get to Toby's third minor trait, his argumentative whistling.

There is reason to believe that Sterne saw that in allowing such formal confusion as this, into which the Dinah story has led his narrator, he was flirting with communicative chaos and thus

with the ruin of his novel. The most immediate sign of his awareness is the complete chapter which divides this long digression's
two main parts. It is a whole chapter of formal clarification dis-
guised as self praise. In it Tristram says:

I was just going . . . to have given you the great outlines of my uncle
Toby's most whimsical character;—when my aunt *Dinah* and the
coachman came a-cross us, and led us a vagary some millions of miles
into the very heart of the planetary system: Notwithstanding all this
you perceive that the drawing of my uncle *Toby's* character went on
gently all the time;—not the great contours of it,—that was impossible,
—but some familiar strokes and faint designations of it, were here and
there touch'd in, as we went along, so that you are much better ac-
quainted with my uncle *Toby* now than you was before.   (72-73)

This does more than admit the confusion: it settles the confusion,
subordinating the Aunt Dinah argument and reasserting the
proper primacy of Toby's character. It re-establishes the integrity
of the digression, which any audience would have come to doubt.
   Another sign of Sterne's awareness of the danger of this confusion is the clarity with which he has pursued Toby's character in
the rest of this digression and his general avoidance of such confusion hereafter. Future digressions will be digressive and pro-
gressive too, explaining a main point of Shandy life, say, by revealing another point of Shandy life or a relevant opinion; and there
will always be in Tristram's digressive practice many conversational freedoms; but the confusion of main and interruptive matter will not be repeated. We might notice in this connection the
late digression Tristram will call "the most puzzled skein of all"
(512-16): this is his weaving into the story of his recent French
travels "a small thread or two" from his earlier French travels.
That small digressive thread Tristram will introduce quite formally to explain why he could go on forever about Auxerre; he
will develop it with perfect lucidity; and he will close it with precision by distinguishing between the threads of his different travels and by taking up again the one which is his chief concern. But
even in this early digressive adventure on Toby's character,
which Sterne wrote when he was still working out his style, he
has finally achieved coherence and allowed Tristram to impress
on his audience a clear and pointed digressive order.

Tristram has generally helped his audience follow his digressions, especially the harder ones, by the emphatic use of paragraphs and chapters. Paragraphs, for instance, divide the exception from the rule in the digressions on sleep and on swearing. Paragraphs divide Tristram's general statement of his troubles and the two points, as an author and as a man, by which he develops it. Paragraphs and transitional paragraphing define the sections of the Preface; and paragraphing sets off the section on Tristram's own travel problems from his opinion of travels in his Invocation (628-31). A complete chapter of clarification divides the digression on Uncle Toby, as we have just seen. A chapter break separates Tristram's statement of the historian's problems from the quotation of his mother's marriage settlement, which led Tristram to make this statement (36-41). And the digression which tells how not to raise creative powers, then how to raise them, and then faces objections is properly parcelled into three chapters. This formal punctuation of digressions does not follow any mechanical rule, and not every paragraph or chapter unit in a digression is so significant as these I have mentioned. However, the patterns of all of Tristram's extended digressions have been sufficiently punctuated for the members of his audience—if they are as attentive as he asks them to be—to have a clear notion of every digression's parts and structure.

Tristram, then, has composed his digressions with great care, using them quite explicitly to help him accommodate his peculiar narrative material to his social situation. We must not be led to miss the care with which he has composed them or their relevance to his discourse by his passing admissions of whimsy or carelessness. Most of these, like his saying that he writes his first sentence and trusts to Almighty God for his second (540), are equivocal, reversible. This most famous admission, for instance, Tristram has followed by saying that it would cure an author of writing any other way to see how orderly and coherent his writing comes out. Nor should we overemphasize Tristram's few artistic failures, such as his very few emotional digressions (224; 451-52), in which he turns his back on his audience, as it were; or his once or twice briefly losing his way (462-63). These flawed passages, all of which are perfectly understandable, should rather underscore the nearly perfect skill with which Tristram has projected his peculiar, oddly involved story as an object of general entertainment and instruction.

III *The Disgressions' Quality and Effect*

But what has Sterne achieved beyond making Tristram's story socially understandable and edifying by working out this hard won solution to a hard pressed problem? He has achieved, to use Tristram's word (614), a "texture," a web of life and opinion, of particular story and general statement which involves the trivial items of Shandy experience with general human truths in a fabric of great richness and density. It is with his opinionative digressions, especially, and with those explanatory ones which contain interweavings of opinion that Tristram has accomplished this texture. We can best approach its nature and value by working through a few examples.

We take, first, Tristram's effort to generalize Walter's response to the news of his son's unlucky misnaming (291-94): Walter "took down his hat with the gentlest movement of limbs, that ever affliction harmonized and attuned together . . . [and] walked composedly . . . to the fish-pond." Tristram has drawn three opinions from this, two from Walter's oddly gentle bearing and one from the pond. The first, that "the different weight, dear Sir, —nay even the different package of two vexations of the same weight,—makes a very wide difference in our manners of bearing and getting through with them," he treats before mentioning Walter's walk to the pond. He has developed it by a particular description of the way he recently bore and got through one of his own vexations by throwing his wig violently at the ceiling; and he further develops it by deriving from that violent action of his a second general opinion: we cannot understand the various peculiar actions by which Nature allows us to relieve our various peculiar griefs. This second opinion gives new meaning to the two odd responses to vexation of Walter and Tristram, taking them both as examples, and refines the first opinion. Thus, Tristram's action is doubly valuable, exemplifying two different if related opinions; and Walter's action is trebly so since it is important as an item of Tristram's story as well as being doubly exemplary.

But the texture of this passage is richer still since the second opinion gives and receives meanings from the matter following it as well as from that which has preceded. It helps explain Walter's walk to the pond, by which it receives further exemplification; for Walter's relief is, like Tristram's wig throwing, another of Nature's mysterious workings; and it is refined and focussed by the general opinion Tristram deduces from Walter's relief, that "there is something, Sir, in fish-ponds . . . under the first disorderly transport of the humours . . . unaccountably becalming." The general truths stated in this passage, then, are variously broadened and refined by their relationship to one another and strengthened by their rootedness in particular Shandy actions; and Walter's action, with which this passage begins and ends, comes, for all its oddity, to represent the variety of mankind's response to grief.

Tristram has had a harder time involving Walter's odd opinion on the importance of free-swinging door hinges with generally relevant truth (203). To manage this, indeed, he has first had to tie Walter's odd notion to Walter's failure to oil the squeaky hinge to his own parlor door. Having asserted that connection, he can rise to a general statement on Walter's nature: "his rhetoric and conduct were at perpetual handy-cuffs." And then he goes on to a universally applicable utterance: "Inconsistent soul that man is . . . his whole life a contradiction to his knowledge!" Walter, in his inconsistency over the door hinge and in his generally inconsistent nature, thus stands once again for all mankind. But Tristram does not stop with Walter. Rather, he applies this universal truth, which he has derived from Walter's peculiar concern with the parlor-door hinge, to his own concern with the very same thing: "The parlour-door shall be mended this reign." He thus unwittingly offers himself as a further example of the inconsistency between man's knowledge and his conduct; and he shows himself to be, at one and the same time, a normal member of the human race and the peculiar Walter Shandy's true and resembling heir.

Tristram works out an extremely ambiguous particular-general texture in his account of Walter's opinion that a man's Christian name determines his destiny (49-56). This, like all of Walter's opinions, seems at first to be in itself both general and particular: it is general in Walter's application of it but totally particular to Walter as a belief, being just one more odd element of Shandy history. In developing it, however, Tristram shakes this interpretation of the opinion. He does this, after first particularizing it with a few names Walter approved and a few he abhorred, by giving Walter's argument for it. This wonderful *ad hominem* argument, which depends on the opponent's admission that he would not name a son Judas, strongly suggests that the opinion is not so peculiar to Walter after all. It leads Tristram on to a general statement about Walter—that he was eloquent and that he had to be so to defend such peculiar opinions as he took up. In explaining Walter's odd opinions, Tristram throws out a warning "to the learned reader against the indiscreet reception of such guests." This discussion of Walter's generally odd opinions leads Tristram back to Walter's opinion of Christian names, which now stands as an example of Walter's peculiarity in his opinions. We must notice the ambiguity here: Walter's opinion of names has been suggested to be, on the one hand, more generally held than is admitted and presented, on the other, as a particular example of Walter's peculiarity in opinions. Tristram does nothing to resolve this ambiguity: "Whether this [that his opinions began in jest and ended in earnest as he has been conjecturing] was the case of the singularity of my father's notions,—or that his judgment, at length, became the dupe of his wit;—or how far, in many of his notions, he might, tho' odd, be absolutely right;—the reader, as he comes at them, shall decide."

Tristram concludes his account of Walter's opinion by giving more names that Walter had fit into his system and by ending with the name Walter most abhorred, Tristram; and thus he draws his reader's attention with tremendous force to those particular events by which he himself came to receive that most hopeless name. But how will the reader take the story now? He may take it as sheer comedy, as an example of much ado about nothing, only remembering that, as Tristram has reminded him, he too is susceptible to such odd opinions and such absurd sorrows. Or he may take his part in Walter's defeat more to heart, admitting that he too worries about names, that he would suffer, some at least, if his son had the name he most abhors affixed to him forever. This passage, then, has given the whole story of Tristram's misnaming an ambiguous general value. It is, at least, an example of Walter's opinions and of the sorrows they led him into. It may be, also, an example of the odd misfortunes all of us, all learned readers anyway, are susceptible to; and it may be, still further, an instance of the miseries all mankind faces because of its (absurd?) concern for names. And, thus, one who came to scoff at Walter's oddity may remain to sympathize. But, as Tristram says, the reader shall decide.

This sort of narrative texture is not peculiar to *Tristram Shandy* in the eighteenth century. *Tom Jones*,[4] which has been shown to share the use of a self-conscious narrator with our novel,[5] also shares this. Fielding's narrator, also, must often stop to explain or generalize an event in his story. He explains the general belief that Tom was born to hang, for instance, by giving three cases of Tom's youthful thievery (77), and explains the high bill Tom got at the inn before Gloucester by giving his readers some maxims on innkeeping (360); he introduces Miss Bridget Allworthy's middle-aged passion for Captain Blifil, again, with some general remarks on the love of middle-aged women, asserting that Miss Bridget will serve as "an example of all these observations" (30). He gives a particular account of Mr. Northerton's escape from the inn where he was confined, first, to clear the character of the sentinel who had been on guard (327) and, second, to explain the compassion of the inn's landlady (328). Fielding's narrator also habitually relates the particular events of his story to general opinions and truths. Sometimes he takes the events merely as occasions, concluding his account of Jones's fight with Thwackum and Blifil, for instance, with the wish that all battles could be settled, as this one has been, without deadly weapons (211). But usually his opinions derive from particular events which reflect on them as examples. In Sophia Western's changing of her hair bow and thus missing her meeting with Tom, the narrator finds a general lesson for all young ladies (236). In the love Sophia felt for Tom after he had saved her from being thrown from her horse, the narrator found particular evidence that bravery endears a man to the hearts of women (152). Jones's drunkenness serves as an example that liquor exaggerates a man's real nature rather than reversing it (199-200); and Jones's gullible belief in Partridge's professions of friendship underlies the narrator's opinion of the two ways by which such incautious trust in others may be overcome (358). Both of these last two opinions, by the way, are

[44]

developed in little bipartite essays, like so many of Tristram Shandy's.

Fielding's novel naturally has something of the texture of Sterne's. Take, for example, the narrator's explanation of Mr. Allworthy's lessening of affection for Tom (97). There are two reasons for it: one is Tom's receiving more affection than Blifil from Mrs. Bridget; the other is Tom's own wildness. The first both explains Mr. Allworthy's feelings and serves as an example of his general habit of mind. The second and, indeed, all those wild actions it introduces not only explain Allworthy's lessening of affection but also exemplify a general lesson, that "Prudence and circumspection are necessary to the best of men." Thus this considerable element of the novel, the story of Tom's wildness, is presented to the reader both as an affective narrative and as a didactic example.

These explanatory and opinionative digressions, which the narrator explicitly describes as digressions (5;224), are often directed explicitly at his reading public, much as Tristram's have been. The example of Tom's wildness is addressed "to all those well-disposed youths who shall hereafter be our readers." The example of Sophia's untimely vanity the narrator has drawn up "only for the sake of the ladies." His report of Mr. Northerton's escape was due to his desire that "the reader" would not damn the sentinel and that "our reader" would not mistake the landlady's compassion. Thus Fielding's narrator has engaged in some of the same digressive practices as Tristram Shandy and for something like the same reason, that is, to attach and to instruct society. Moreover, he has achieved a similar, if not as thick and complex, a discursive texture as Tristram has.

The texture in *Tristram Shandy* is thicker partly because Sterne's narrator must include himself in his story, being the last member of the family he is describing, whereas Fielding's narrator can maintain a kind of divine distance from his. More important than this is the difference in the two narrators' materials. The particular characters and events of *Tom Jones* are so typical of mankind that the connection between them and general human nature is broad and firm. In asserting it, Fielding's narrator needed merely to weave the simple, sturdy fabric he has woven. But Tristram has had to bind his general lessons and applications to an almost impossibly peculiar and atypical narrative; and this has required of him the imaginative variety and dexterity that we have been examining.

The texture of Tristram's discourse is thicker, finally, because Tristram has attempted to involve all possible elements of society in it as deeply as he could (7). Fielding's narrator wished to give a generally true account of human nature to those who could relish it (1-3). He confidently dismissed those who could not (1;216-217), willing to satisfy himself, if necessary, with fit audience though few. He had, therefore, no need of pointed attentions or elaborate courtesies. But Tristram, with his desire to keep all segments of society vividly and personally attentive, has had "to consult everyone a little in his turn" (7). This explains the pointedness and the variety of his vast system of explanations, entertainments, and opinions.

Every reader will determine for himself the effect of Tristram's discursive texture of life and opinions, as Tristram has often acknowledged (7-8;11;48-50;53;56-57;108-09;202-03). But attentive readers may well find themselves so involved that "nothing which has touched [Tristram] will be thought trifling in its nature, or tedious in its telling" (11)—just as Tristram hoped they would. They may come to feel that every most peculiar Shandy item is pregnant with general truth and that every general truth is radiant with life. As they weigh Walter's opinions of noses and names and follow his defeats; as they weigh Toby's opinions of marriage and love and follow the failure of his courtship; as they weigh Tristram's opinions on literature and follow his hopeless struggle to describe his whole life: sensitive readers may feel the absurd peculiarity of their own opinions and the narrow scope of all human actions.

CHAPTER 4

Tristram's Tragicomical Transformation

THE facts of Tristram Shandy's private life are tragic. His childhood misfortunes have made certain his family's doom; he is his family's sole survivor; and with his approaching death his family will become extinct. Thus Tristram's past is pitiful, his present desolate, and his future hopeless. To present this tragic history to polite society, however, he must redeem its misery and pain—transform it into something charming and gay. This tragicomical transformation which Tristram has worked on his life story is our present subject.

I *Tristram's Tragic Vision*

We had best begin it, however, by establishing the depth and consistency of Tristram's tragic vision. We must be clear on that to appreciate his comic wizardry. Tristram's vision of the forces underlying his life, which we may discuss as death, chance, and time, is, as must now be shown, perfectly consonant with the terrible effects they have had on him. It is that vision, that understanding, which all men share in their hearts: death is inevitable and incalculable; chance and time are intransigent in their courses and largely unopposable in their workings.

The shadow of death, as W. B. C. Watkins has seen,[1] broods over this novel. Sterne has generally focussed it, however, not on the Shandys but on their acquaintance—on Yorick, with whom its presence was first asserted (27-34), on LeFever (416-26), and on Corporal Trim (451-52). But Sterne has allowed Tristram to reveal Shandy deaths too. Great-aunt Dinah's death, implied by the legacy she left Walter (337), has been elsewhere explicitly admitted (69;490). Tristram also reports the death of his older brother Bobby (336). It was on the occasion of Bobby's death, we may recall, that Walter made his eloquent speech on human mortality

(353-57) and Trim his more eloquent gesture—by dropping his hat "as if a lump of clay had been kneaded into the crown of it" (362). Tristram acknowledges obliquely the death of his mother (472); and he has revealed Uncle Toby's death (451-52) by glancing into the great gap of his life, about 1723-59, which he never gets around to filling in. There are signs that Tristram's father also died in this dark chasm of Tristram's unrecorded time. Most obvious are Walter's uncertain health and advanced age way back at the time of Tristram's conception in 1718 (8;296-98;333) and Tristram's present control of the Shandy estate (203;204). We may take Tristram's swearing by his father's ashes (56) as an oblique confirmation of Walter's death. Tristram's failure to address his father or, indeed, any of his family in his voluminous discourse strongly validates these admissions and signs; and it suggests, overwhelmingly, that Tristram is the lone survivor of his family.

As Tristram's words make increasingly clear, death must soon take him too. Tristram admits, for one thing, that he is suffering from a dreadful disease. He talks of his "vile asthma" (10;545), for instance, and discovers his figure to be the "very thin" one of a wasted consumptive (480;493). He also complains of a cough (479) which has cost him great losses of blood (545;627). These suggestions of maturing illness are, significantly, most numerous in the novel's last three volumes. None of them shatters the surface of Tristram's gaiety, not even this most terrible one of all: "To this hour art thou not tormented with the vile asthma thou gattest in skating against the wind in *Flanders?* and is it but two months ago, that in a fit of laughter, on seeing a cardinal make water like a quirister (with both hands) thou brakest a vessel in thy lungs, whereby, in two hours, thou lost as many quarts of blood; and hadst thou lost as much more, did not the faculty tell thee—it would have amounted to a gallon?—" (545). But Tristram's meaning, that he "must be cut off in the midst of [his] days" (495), is plain. Sterne has focussed all these suggestions of mortal illness by leading his hero in Volume VII on a headlong and extensive flight from death.

He has completed the pattern of Tristram's encroaching mortality in Volume IX. Such admissions as that in the apostrophe to

Jenny, in which Tristram sees the "eternal separation which we are shortly to make" (610-11), furnish explicit evidence of death's imminent action. More pervasive in its suggestiveness, however, is Tristram's winding up in this volume of all his public commitments. The completion of Toby's amours, so recently threatened with eternal interruption, is only the most obvious element in this winding up. In Volume IX, as Wayne Booth has shown,[2] Tristram tells all he has promised to tell and promises no more. Sterne clinches the impression of conclusion at the volume's end with Toby's return to the Shandy circle and with Yorick's parting quip, the equivocal epitome of Tristram's whole equivocal discourse. Tristram's so often insisting that he would go on writing until his death (74;162;166;285-86;479) heightens the mortal meaning of this rounding off. The mere fact of Tristram's concluding in only one volume—how decisive this must have seemed to Sterne's first readers who had been following Tristram's life over the years (from 1759 to 1767) in two volume installments. Readers nowadays must do without this sign; but Sterne has given us enough evidence to see that Volume IX concludes Tristram's unlucky life and to understand what the conclusion of this life—which to be comprehensive was commenced *ab ovo*—must be.

Sterne has imposed the power of chance on his novel, if any thing, more forcefully than he has that of death. Tristram calls this power by many names besides "chance" (279-81;382;567; 599): there are "circumstances" (158;376;575;576), "fortune" and its variants (4;7;8;25;36;41;167;186;etc.), "accident" (6;10; 320;383;578), "destiny" (281;314), and various forms of "luck" (26;277;280;334). Sometimes Tristram has personified this force as "the Fates" (552), "the destinies" (41;118;314), or Fortune that "ungracious Duchess" (10); and sometimes he uses odd, evocative expressions like "cross-purposes" (55), "cross reckonings" (277), "tide of little evils and distresses" (215), and "jerks and hard jostlings" (278). But, whatever he calls it, Tristram accepts it as mere happenstance, as the accidental grinding on of events: "the circumstances with which everything in this world is begirt, give everything in this world its size and shape" (158). Tristram never attempts to make an abstract judgment on chance, sometimes laying its workings to heaven (296;608), and sometimes to

a malignant spirit (56); but he has richly and pointedly acknowledged its power over his and his family's life.

Chance, as Tristram recognizes it, seems especially to have
thwarted Walter Shandy. Walter believed that he could head off
chance and determine the course of events; and he put the belief
in practice on the occasions of Tristram's begetting, birth, christening, and education. But, as Tristram's detailed report of these
efforts has shown, chance upset Walter at every point. Such things
as Mrs. Shandy's unlucky association of ideas, Dr. Slop's cut thumb,
the curate's being named Tristram, to point out a few links in the
chains of chance, ruined each of Walter's efforts. None of his
losses, however, upset Walter's hope: each loss merely set him on
a new project and a new struggle: "he had lost my brother *Bobby*
entirely,—he had lost, by his own computation, full three-fourths
of me—that is, he had been unfortunate in his three first great
casts for me—my geniture, nose, and name,—there was but this
one left" (372), Tristram's education. And Walter set out with
typical scholarly zeal to make the best of this last chance by
composing his *Tristrapædia*. Even when that was given up, at the
time of Tristram's window-sash accident, Walter kept on planning.
The last we see of him, he is trying to redeem all with a scholasti-
cally designed pair of breeches. None of his misfortunes makes
Walter give up his idea that with study and attention he can
avoid evil luck or, at least, overbalance it (278-79;372). But, in
reporting Walter's defeats, Tristram shows clearly that he does
not agree with Walter.

The only misfortune the infant Tristram suffered that Walter
had no part in was "Susannah's accident" (432;433) with the window-sash. Trim, who had cut down the sash weight, and Toby,
who gave him his orders, both tried to take the responsibility for
it; but the chamber maid who neglected to put the ******* ***
back under Tristram's bed was as guilty as anyone. The truth is,
of course, that none of them is responsible any more than Count
Solmes was responsible, by losing the battle at Steenkirk, for the
wound Trim suffered at Landen. It was pure accident, pure
chance—unforeseeable and unavoidable by the powers and proj-
ects of men. In this carefully detailed sequence of events, as in
all those that led to his infant misfortunes, Tristram has seen and
has made us see that it was chance or circumstance or what E. M.

Forster has called the god Muddle[3]—and not his parents or his uncle or their servants—that brought about his tragedy.

The adult Tristram is more obviously the subject of chance than his father was; and he knows it. He must say, as his hopefully active father never would, that the Fates foreknew everything (522) and, more pointedly still, that he was "doomed by marriage-articles to have my nose squeezed as flat to my face, as if the destinies had spun me without one" (41) and doomed further by "the mere loss, or rather compression of this one single member" to the whole "train of vexatious disappointments" which has pursued him through life (166). Walter's hopes, we come to see, were due to his natural human ignorance of the future: each coming event, he thought, might be governed if he took care. But Tristram, who looks back on the whole system of his misfortunes, cannot be fooled. He sees, moreover, that the effects of chance on his infant body have completely determined his future life; he is, as he admits, "the continual sport of . . . fortune" (10;166). These effects, for all their seeming triviality, have blocked him, somehow, from all the chances for action—from such things as political advancement or business gains or a productive marriage—that men normally enjoy. Sterne has powerfully but tactfully underscored this inaction by never showing Tristram engaged in such normal human endeavors: except for a couple of extremely ambiguous adventures, Tristram only talks and teases. A continuous irony of Tristram's "Life" is that he has no life to tell of—no such actions and achievements and plans as we generally mean by life.

Time's presence in Tristram's discourse is more various than chance's; but its terrible power over Tristram's and his family's life has been, finally, as clearly and even more pervasively asserted. Sterne has darkened both the Shandy past and Tristram's present with signs of the inevitable working of time. Some of these signs, such as that of worn and decaying and wasted items, we find in both these elements of Tristram's discourse. In the Shandy past, Tristram discovers balding heads, ruined jackboots, worn out breeches, dusty wigs, weedy greens, and a broken hinge, all of which bespeak time's inevitable eviction from their proper places of the elder Shandys. Some of these items, such as the hinge and the weedy green, Tristram has now taken over in his turn.

Other signs of time's might—such as Tristram's own spidery legs, his Jenny's graying locks, and his variously interrupted writings—focus on Tristram alone.

He has made explicit the irrevocable turning of time these signs suggest by his many references to dates and chronology—both past and present. He notes, for instance, that Mrs. Shandy's fruitless trip to London came in the latter end of September, 1717 (41), that she conceived him on the first Sunday night in March 1718 (8), and that she bore him on November 5 (9). We know many other dates of his story too and also many spaces of time: we know that the LeFever affair came about seven years before Walter Shandy moved into the country (416), for instance, and that Tristram was begot thirteen months after the fruitless London trip (43). Present times are similarly acknowledged: Tristram has reported that it is March 9, 1759, early in his writing (44) and August 12, 1766, toward its close (600). One particularly subtle way in which Tristram reflects time's wasteful passage is his recognition of changes in styles of dress—from the low-cut pockets of George the First's time (159), and from the long nightshifts of King William's and Queen Anne's reigns (547). One way and another, then, Tristram has acknowledged time and shown how its minutes (162;357-58;363;408;619), hours (65;283;302), months (7ff;403), and years (88-89;285;625) have visited the Shandys with cramped backs, squeezed wigs, ruined hopes, and, of course, distant and imminent deaths. Tristram has given us, indeed, an extensive chronological account of Shandy life which is, as Theodore Baird has shown,[4] remarkably detailed and precise.

Tristram's true representation of his story's sequences underscores this chronological exactitude: Tristram's conception precedes his birth; his birth precedes his christening as he insists it must (56); and that precedes his childhood mutilation. Tristram does rearrange some of his story's events: he tells about his mutilation before telling about Trim's removal of the sash weight that caused it, for instance; he tells about his unlucky beginnings before he tells about the actually earlier events of Uncle Toby's amours; and he describes Yorick's death before he tells of Yorick's several contacts with his family. But Tristram never misrepresents or ignores the actual order of things—as Molly Bloom does in her private reverie. And he recounts many elements of his story, such

as the stages of Walter's anger at his wife (42) and the development of Toby's hobbyhorse (446), in strict sequential form. The
whole discourse proceeds, as has been widely seen, in three great
sequential thrusts of action, which none of Tristram's dodges or
digressions is allowed to blur.

We have still not exhausted the impress of time on the world
of the Shandys: Walter and Toby each had a special difficulty with
time. The active Walter had trouble getting things done on time.
Tristram, who has been trying to explain Walter's slow progress in
the *Tristrapædia*, for instance, continues: "he was three years and
something more, indefatigably at work, and at last, had scarce
compleated, by his own reckoning, one half of his undertaking:
the misfortune was, that I was all that time totally neglected and
abandoned to my mother; and what was almost as bad, by the
very delay, the first part of the work, upon which my father had
spent the most of his pains, was rendered entirely useless,—every
day a page or two became of no consequence" (375). Walter has
the same trouble getting his letter of amatory advice done in
time for it to serve Toby (593) and getting his breeches on in
time to attend Tristram's christening (287). The inactive Toby
never tried to meet such temporal deadlines as these, but he had a
trouble of his own: he often confused the actually diverse epochs
of his life. Here, for instance, he and Trim are standing in the
Shandy parlor discussing the effect of given names on character:

. . . had my name been *Alexander,* I could have done no more at
Namur than my duty—Bless your honour! cried *Trim,* advancing three
steps as he spoke, does a man think of his christian name when he
goes upon the attack?—Or when he stands in the trench, *Trim?* cried
my uncle *Toby,* looking firm—Or when he enters a breach? said *Trim,*
pushing in between two chairs—Or forces the lines? cried my uncle,
rising up, and pushing his crutch like a pike—Or facing a platoon, cried
Trim, presenting his stick like a firelock—Or when he marches up the
glacis, cried my uncle *Toby,* looking warm and setting his foot upon
his stool.   (295)

The effect here, as in similar passages (380-81;464-65), arises
from the actual difference Tristram sees and makes us see between time past and time present. Our laughter reflects our recognition that the mind cannot transform a footstool into a glacis,

that one cannot by imagination change his present situation or call back yesterday. With these different temporal troubles of his great forebears Tristram defines the two qualities of time that all mortals know and endure: its furious speed and its intransigence.

It is easy to see why the Shandy historian must reveal his father and his uncle in the chains of time when we remember his constant desire to impress them as truly as he can upon the consciousness of society. If he were to ignore or confuse the temporal sequence of Walter's struggles for himself and of Toby's amours, he would be misrepresenting Walter and Toby. To describe Walter's ambitions truly, for instance, Tristram must make it clear that Walter planned to name him Trismegistus only after his conception and his birth had turned out badly; and, to report Toby's soldierly modesty aright, he must show that Toby attacked Mrs. Wadman only after the peace of Utrecht had relieved him from his normal military duties and after Mrs. Wadman had repeatedly invaded his bowling green.

One may object here that Tristram, for all these signs of time's power, has yet given Walter and Toby a vast leisure and a freedom from time's grossest effects. This is true, but it is not due to any actual temporal immunity they enjoy (not even in Tristram's memory) but, rather, to their dedicated heir's tremendous temporal expense and to his temporal limitations:

> I am this month one whole year older than I was this time twelve-month; and having got, as you perceive, almost into the middle of my fourth volume—and no farther than to my first day's life—'tis demonstrative that I have three hundred and sixty-four days more life to write just now, than when I first set out; so that instead of advancing, as a common writer, in my work with what I have been doing at it—on the contrary, I am just thrown so many volumes back—
>
> .   .   .   .
>
> As for the proposal of twelve volumes a year, or a volume a month, it no way alters my prospect—write as I will, and rush as I may into the middle of things, as *Horace* advises,—I shall never overtake myself—whipp'd and driven to the last pinch, at the worst I shall have one day the start of my pen—and one day is enough for two volumes—and two volumes will be enough for one year.—(285-86)

Tristram has thus sacrificed three hundred and sixty-four of his waning days to give Walter and Toby one day of apparently limitless being. This three hundred and sixty-four to one expense of Tristram's also assures them of never facing death in his story. They enjoy a narrative ease and an apparent immortality, then, because Tristram's art is long and his life is short.

But there is nothing to give Tristram even the illusion of temporal freedom. He openly acknowledges time's triumphant motion and its absolute stiffness, especially over his discursive efforts. He once admits, for instance, that "my honour has lain bleeding [on account of two missing chapters] this half hour" (632) and, again, that time's pressure has made him completely forget his mother, whom he had meant to leave stooping by the parlor door for only five minutes (357-58;367). He has begun the story of Le-Fever by regretting that the occasion for letting Trim tell it is past and lost (416). And he faces a new set of narrative problems, at another time, with comic desperation: "I have a hundred difficulties which I have promised to clear up, and a thousand distresses and domestic misadventures crouding in upon me thick and three-fold, one upon the neck of another" (235). Tristram, the writer, then, richly and variously admits that "time presses upon me" (397;336;378).

He makes few references to time's power over his life, but those he does make are severe and decisive. We may sense Tristram's personal implication in his invocation to Janatone, who carries "the principles of change within [her] frame," and, "considering the chances of a transitory life," may "go off like a flower" (490). In the apostrophe to Jenny, Tristram explicitly includes himself: "Time wastes too fast: every letter I trace tells me with what rapidity Life follows my pen; the days and hours of it, more precious, my dear *Jenny!* than the rubies about thy neck, are flying over our heads like light clouds of a windy day, never to return more—every thing presses on—whilst thou art twisting that lock, —see! it grows grey; and every time I kiss thy hand to bid adieu, and every absence which follows it, are preludes to that eternal separation which we are shortly to make.—[¶]—Heaven have mercy upon us both!" (610-11).

At the beginning of his discourse Tristram's power as a writer seemed to impregnate and fortify the man: "Digressions, incontestably, are the sunshine;—they are the life, the soul of reading; —take them out of this book for instance,—you might as well take the book along with them;—one cold eternal winter would reign in every page of it; restore them to the writer;—he steps forth like a bridegroom,—bids All hail; brings in variety, and forbids the appetite to fail" (73). Toward its close the process is reversed, and the writer partakes of the man's temporal enthrallment. At Chapter Twelve of Volume IX Tristram started out on "a good frisky" digression, but by Chapter Fifteen he has found his time has run out: "The fifteenth chapter is come at last; and brings nothing with it but a sad signature of 'How our pleasures slip from under us in this world;' [¶] For in talking of my digression—I declare before heaven I have made it" (618).

Death, chance, and time, then, brood over Tristram's efforts and Tristram's days with at least as much power as they do over other men. Death, which has taken all the other Shandys, is soon to take him; chance, which ruined Walter's familial ambitions, has curtailed Tristram's life; and time, which has borne Tristram irrevocably from those he loves, now sweeps him toward death. But for all that, Tristram's circumstantial account of these forces and their dreadful Shandy effects is comical and gay. We must now try to see how he managed to make it so.

II   Tristram's Comical Transformation

He has been able to keep Shandy deaths from marring his account chiefly through organization. Mrs. Shandy, Walter, Toby, and Trim have died in the great gap of unrecorded time between Tristram's early misfortunes (about 1717-24) and his first taking pen in hand (about 1759). His slow narrative progress and what we may call his untimely death have preserved the gap and thus relieved Tristram of the painful narrative confrontations these deaths would have caused him. His own death has been avoided simply by Sterne's making the discourse entirely Tristram's work: a writer cannot report his own demise. Thus all the deaths that would disturb Tristram's comic tone are neatly dodged.

This organizational legerdemain has allowed Tristram to mention the deaths of his major figures equivocally, apprising us of their mortal departures without making a point of them. Walter Shandy's age and infirmity, for instance, Tristram has clearly informed us of, but only as explanations of his sexual moderation. We know that he was between fifty and sixty years old (8) and that he was troubled with chills and sciatica (9;314-15) as far back as Tristram's conception. But Tristram so presents these indications of encroaching mortality as to direct society's mind entirely toward Walter's sexual activity and potency and never toward his death. These facts about Walter thus seem merely to be elements in the equivocally bawdy fabric of Tristram's talk. Toby's weakness and aging—his increased weight (601), his balding head (591), and the lingering signs of his wound (626-37)—seem, likewise, to be chiefly relevant to the story of his amours. When Tristram tells us of Toby's death (452), we are not surprised; but we would never have thought of it on our own. This mortal announcement is still further equivocated: Tristram has faced it less as a terrible event of his past life than as a difficult problem in his future writing. It is one, as Sterne well knew, that his social entertainer must never live to tackle.

Tristram has also reduced the tragic effects of those deaths he has described. The deaths of Bobby Shandy and LeFever, for instance, have been softened by Tristram's giving these figures almost no presence in his story: Bobby is merely a lad of wonderful slow parts; and Le Fever is, as his name informs us, just a fever. The pity of Bobby's death has been further dissolved with Walter Shandy's heart-easing eloquence (350-57). Yorick's death may seem excessive, dangerously sentimental, for all the wit and humor of its telling; but its emotional power has also been reduced—chiefly by Yorick's appearing alive and well later on in Tristram's discourse and by his becoming dear to us only after his death is safely behind him. It may be worthwhile to notice that he, whose death virtually opened Tristram's story, is the one who makes its closing comment, its last jest.

Tristram's own impending death is variously equivocated. Tristram never thinks of it by itself; it is merely the end of his writing (74;286;479) or the cause of a speedy southern trip (479ff). Sometimes he has revealed his mortality, as he did Walter's and Toby's, as a matter of bawdry: he plans to recover from an ambiguously unlucky adventure with Jenny, for instance, by drinking goat's whey, which will, incidentally, lengthen his life by seven years (517-18). Some diversion interrupts even the most direct references to his impending death: they may end in jests against papistry, which would send him by oil rather than water (527), or against his audience, for whose disapproval of his poignant fare-well to Jenny he would not give a groat (611). Death, then, which has pervaded Tristram's story and his life, is never oppressive. Tristram has managed to assert its many victories and to imply its final victory without clouding his entertaining discourse.

Chance and its workings have posed a harder problem. Since death was merely a set of isolated moments, Tristram could easily dodge its sterner manifestations; but chance dwells in the long toils of time. Moreover, chance has borne decisively on those events which Tristram must tell about to account for his life. Although Tristram's death and the death of the Shandy family were implied in Tristram's conception, birth, christening, and mutilation, its immediate presence did not cloud their telling; but chance has permeated them. Thus no organizational tricks could save Tristram from admitting the terrible power of chance over his infancy. He has had, instead, to equivocate it; and he has done so variously.

Tristram has given chance's workings on himself a comic turn, first of all, by his presentation of his father, the Shandy champion. The very fact that Walter is a philosopher, not a statesman or a soldier, is the first comic element in his struggles. A philosopher, as we generally think of him, is one who searches after immutable truths, who lives in an ivory tower. He never ventures into the world of actions and events, into the world of chance and chances; he stands apart devoting himself to those studies which chance cannot endanger. Thus Walter's philosophical activity, his effort to force his studies on the shapeless flow of events, will seem outlandish and absurd—at least to all those practical men, the lawyers, doctors, actors, critics, churchmen, and politicians, who make up much of Tristram's audience.

Tristram has been able to underscore Walter's absurd activity, moreover, with his account of Uncle Toby. Toby's absurdity is the perfect contrast to Walter's since Toby is a passive, unambitious soldier. Toby, who took everything as it happened, was content to do his duty in war and to smoke his pipe in peace. "There is no cause but one," he tells Walter, "why one man's nose is longer than another's, but because that God pleases to have it so" (240). Having thus consigned the chances of this world to God, the pious Toby would not think of tampering. If we were to set up plans in opposition to God's, Toby says, heaven's artillery "would batter [them] . . . about our ears" (296). When Walter's plans for Tristram's nose were battered down and the distraught father was wondering how he might bear up his spirits and counterbalance his bad luck, Toby assured him: "'Tis by the assistance of Almighty God . . . 'tis not from our own strength" (277). But, of course, his words fell on deaf ears.

The humor of Toby's bowling-green campaigns comes in good part from their strict removal from pretentious action. Toby, who was a perfect soldier except in essence—the essence of war being its challenge of present circumstances to change the course of the future—always ordered his battles to go as they had gone, planning nothing and effecting nothing. Toby had too high an opinion of military skill to admit that battles were entirely predestined (608), but he himself never worried about their courses: at home and abroad, Captain Shandy was satisfied to do his duty (295). By his complacent presence and his passive skepticism, Toby makes, quite unintentionally, a running satire on all of Walter's plans and actions. Toby's simple responses to the philosophical consideration of Tristram's christening (277;279;298), for instance, bring out the practical futility of such lucubrations; and his whistling of "Lillabullero" again and again casts a satiric cloud over Walter's philosophical plans. How absurd it is for the philosopher to take the field when the soldier has folded his hands.

Another element to the absurdity of Walter's philosophical activity is his isolation, his removal from the actions he wants to direct. The events by which Tristram's nose was compressed and his name lost, like those that led to his mutilation, can be unlinked without any reference to Walter: he waited below stairs—much of the time asleep—while Mrs. Shandy, the midwife, Dr. Slop, and others attended to Tristram's birth. He came too late to oversee the christening and left too soon to discover his defeat. Susannah's flippant response to Walter's inquiry about the goings on at Tristram's birth (284-85), Walter's most ambitious action, underscores his absurd removal from the actual center of events. The joke is heightened by the fact that those actually present were, by chance, perfectly calculated to bring on Walter's misfortunes. Susannah, with her leaky memory, her confident carelessness, her prejudices and prudery, is a mere floating system of bad

Shandy luck. Even the richer character, Slop, with his loose forceps, his cut thumb, and his truculent papistry, is largely a bolting
hutch of Shandy misfortune. Walter Shandy, so removed from the
actions he would direct and so represented at them as he has
been, is an obvious target for laughter.

The misfortunes he suffers are laughable, moreover, in their
seeming triviality. If the points for which Walter planned with
such concern had seemed important—if, that is, something like
his or Tristram's life had seemed to be at stake—society could
hardly have laughed at the story however ridiculous were Walter's measures. A nose, a name, a pair of breeches, and even a
conception give a properly trivial first impression. The fact that
none of these Shandy mischances leads to any immediate danger
allows Tristram, even while admitting their deadly implications,
to keep them light. One hardly recognizes that personal desolation and family extinction can be derived from such trivial things
as an odd marriage article, a loose rivet, a curate's being named
Tristram, or a misplaced chamber pot. The fact that Tristram's
trivial accidents may also be socially unmentionable further les-
sens their tragic impact. The nose-penis equivocation, for instance,
although Tristram often asserts its tragic side, always leaves the
polite members of Tristram's audience too concerned with their
own titillations or with the confusions of their prudish neighbors
(or with both of these) to attend to Tristram's tragic destiny.
Tristram equivocates the tragic value of the window-sash accident in the same way, by introducing it, not chiefly as a terrible
event in his life, but as one which he fears he cannot tell with decency. Tristram has thus been able to disguise Walter's losses and
his own misfortunes as items of trivial bawdiness.

Tristram has given the tragic powers of time a different but an
equally effective transformation. The effects of time on the
Shandy past, as we have already suggested, are softened by Tristram's method of narration. By focussing on a very few Shandy
situations and by giving them a full, leisurely report, he has surrounded Toby and Walter with an aura of timelessness. Because
we see them unchanging in our relatively long acquaintance with
them, we come to think of them as unchanging. We forget what
Tristram has clearly told us: that we are seeing them on only a
few days from one rather narrow segment of their lives. We see

both brothers extensively on the day of Tristram's birth; we see them on the day, a few years later, when he was mutilated, and over several days, a few years earlier, when Toby courted Mrs. Wadman. There are only the briefest glimpses from other stages of their lives (459-62;512-15;578-79). No wonder we think of them as eternally the same, even though Tristram has made it clear by admitting the gaps in his story and by giving us brief glimpses of the rest of their lives, that Walter and Toby were young once and that they came to die.

The expressive effect of this expansive method of narration is heightened by a few odd elements in Tristram's narrative organization. By describing Yorick's part in his life after he has described Yorick's death, for instance, Tristram seems to have cancelled out Yorick's mortality. Likewise, by describing Toby's amours (an event of around 1713) after finishing with his own early life (1718-24), he is able to wipe the knowledge of his own bad luck from Toby's and Walter's minds and to leave them, at the close of his discourse, in the generally happy family circle which his beginnings would (did) interrupt. Tristram, then, has so told and so organized his life story as to give us the impression of its major participants as unchanging and as unchangingly comfortable even though he never invites us to confuse this impression with reality.

But this illusion of leisure which Tristram has bestowed on Walter and Toby only focusses his readers' attention more acutely on his own tremendous hurry and limitations. No matter how he organizes his episodes, each one takes much longer to describe than it did to happen;[5] each one, whether it describes a recent event or one of long ago, cuts into his waning share of days. Every reference he makes to this temporal relationship between his family's doings and his writing leads him and his audience to the certainty that he will reach the end of his days having told about only a fraction of them. However, this way of admitting time's power over his own life is also a way of softening his audience's sense of it. It saves him from admitting time's effects on his body and on his hopes while yet representing it truly, allowing him to turn our attention merely to confused sentences, misplaced episodes, and lost narrative and digressive occasions. The lost chance for Trim's telling the story of LeFever (415-16), and the tangled sentence (462-63) and crooked volumes (473-75) which he cannot go back and straighten admit Tristram's feeling of time's power and at the same time transform it by emphasizing not its personal, but its discursive effect. These admissions and others, such as his failure to get to things he especially wants to tell (337), his not having reached things he should already be past (235), and his inability to describe at once concurrent actions in the Shandy parlor and the Shandy kitchen (357-58;367), all make us think, "poor Tristram, he can't keep up with his story," and not, "poor Tristram, his time is running out." By describing himself thus, Tristram presents himself as a comic victim rather than as a tragic sufferer of time's dreadful working.

There are, of course, admissions of time's power over Tristram besides these—direct admissions of its effect on his life, each of which has had to be given its own comical turn. The flight from death, an explicit sign that Tristram "must be cut off in the midst of my days," is turned into a combination French romp and travel satire. His hurry is just a cue for amusingly brief and confused meetings with French men and women (487-88;491; etc.) and for absurdly nonexperiential descriptions of French points of interest (484-86;489-90;499-501; etc.). The hurry almost never stands out for what it is: Tristram's desperate dodge of time's sweeping scythe. The admission in his apostrophe to Jenny (610-11), again, and his sudden realization of "How our pleasures slip from under us in this world," which his lost chance for a digression has brought home to him (618), Tristram disperses in flirts at his audience. Thus in handling time, as in handling chance, Tristram admits its power over him without ever letting us dwell on that power's tragic implications.

Nothing better shows Tristram's success in transforming the tragic power of time than the words of some of Sterne's most thoughtful critics. John Traugott, who sometimes speaks of a "double reality of time" in *Tristram Shandy*, seems most happy with the notion of an "ironic no-time." [6] This agrees with the belief in Tristram's timelessness expressed by Dorothy Van Ghent[7] and B. H. Lehmann.[8] These two critics, it is true, argue from the remarkable belief that Tristram is not a public entertainer, but an unzipped and undisciplined mind; still, their feeling about time in the novel shows how successfully Tristram has transformed its tragic presence. W. B. C. Watkins, although he noticed some signs of time the destroyer, has also settled on the Joycean notion of an internal timelessness.[9] He seems to have done this because of confusing Tristram Shandy, the hard-pressed public entertainer, with Laurence Sterne, the omnipotent literary artist. However, his ability to imagine Tristram's temporal situation as "relative, dependent upon the imagination and the point of view of the individual consciousness," shows again how deceptively Tristram has transformed his time's hard facts. Arthur Cash, who avoided both the unzipped mind mistake and the Tristram-Laurence confusion, has also succumbed to this transformation.[10] Other critics, however, have read down through it to Tristram's temporal reality: Alice Green Fredman, for instance, writes that Tristram is aware of limitations to his existence; [11] and Alan Mc-Killop says that Sterne's novel presents "the direct intractable experience of time." [12] Putting McKillop's statement with that of Watkins, we may say that there is a double impression of time in *Tristram Shandy:* there is Tristram's comic equivocation of time, and there is time itself. Tristram has been no more able to reverse time's actual power than any man; but he has given it a wonderfully effective social disguise.

So far we have discussed chiefly Tristram's use of organization and of equivocation to give the pitiful facts of his life a comic telling. There is one other major element in his tragicomical transformation: this is his detachment from his narrative materials. This discursive distance is based, of course, on Tristram's actual temporal distance. Tristram looks back to his story's great actions over a great gap of unrecorded time (from about 1759 to about 1724 and before)—as he never lets us forget. Sometimes he defines this gap humorously by seeming to ignore it, by calling across it to the long dead Trim and Toby (451-52), or by saying that he wants swaddling (235). The obvious difference between the two Tristrams—the one a mute infant or bawling child, the other a loquacious gentleman—keeps us constantly aware of the time that divides them. When Tristram says, at the close of the window-sash affair, "Let us leave if possible myself:—But 'tis impossible,—I must go with you to the end of the work" (442), he is giving us one last reminder, through his double presence, of the great gap of time which separates him from his life's material.

Tristram has added to our sense of this separation by making it clear that he knows the end of all his stories. He has told us about Toby's shock from the widow Wadman even before he takes up that old story (101); and his book's title page has prepared us for the unlucky conclusion of Walter's plan to name him Trismegistus.

This carefully preserved sense of temporal detachment makes every event Tristram describes an old story, a winter's tale, whose dramatic urgency has long ago evaporated. It makes natural Tristram's speaking of his nosemashing as Walter's misfortune (292; 296), not his own; and his calling his unlucky circumcision "Susannah's accident" (432;433). Tristram's detachment from these events is, however, not one of indifference; it is, rather, the attitude of the dedicated scholar and teacher. Tristram sees himself as "a man of erudition" (85) who is deeply concerned with "scientific research" (5). "My way," he tells society, "is ever to point out to the curious, different tracts of investigation, to come at the first springs of the events I tell . . . with the officious humility of a heart devoted to the assistance merely of the inquisitive;—to them I write,—and by them I shall be read,—if any such reading as this could be supposed to hold out so long, to the very end of the world" (66). A work so conceived and composed is naturally one "of strict morality and close reasoning" (218) which demands its audience's close attention (56-57).

Tristram, in accordance with these intentions, makes very few sincere claims on his audience's sympathy (55;359), but he makes many claims on their curiosity and attention. He presents Uncle Toby's amours to his listeners as "one of the most compleat systems, both of the elementary and the practical part of love and love-making" (466). He takes great pains, again, to give them the exact date of his conception, saying that it is "by the bye [that he will] . . . carry . . . the effects with me to my grave" (8-9). This pervasive detachment toward his life makes Tristram's few flashes of emotion (90;451-52) strangely moving: they are, like Toby's moments of eloquence, remarkable exceptions. But this detachment is chiefly important to Tristram as a device for making his pitiful life socially entertaining.

This cool detachment makes natural Tristram's high-handed organization of his life's events and his playful equivocation of its substance—those other devices by which he has transformed its tragedies. This detachment may be thought, moreover, to induce a like attitude in his listeners, freeing them from the sympathetic involvements which might depress their spirits and blind their eyes. Madam and Sir, seeing Tristram's ease before his misfortunes, may very well feel easy themselves.

Tristram has not been able to treat his present situation with the same detachment, of course, nor has Sterne wanted him to. With Tristram's passing admissions of recent great losses of blood (545;627), with his headlong flight from death, with his frustrated adventure with Jenny (517-18), and with his apostrophe to her (610-11), Sterne has made sure that Tristram's audience will be able to infer the personal tragedy which Tristram has transformed so deceptively. Tristram has also equivocated these present signs of his tragedy, seasoning them with comedy, so that nothing disrupts his gay social entertainment. But they should still remind us that Tristram's discourse, in its total evocative dimension, is not a comedy but, as Tristram has admitted (512), a "tragicomical . . . contexture." Of course, each reader must decide for himself whether to laugh or to cry. Those who respond to Tristram's explicit intention, which was to fence against the infirmities of life with mirth (3;301-02), will take it, finally, as a comedy. But it is one, as they should all see, that Tristram has derived from the most pitiful, dreary, and unlikely materials.

CHAPTER 5

Tristram's Trial by Prudery

DESPITE the continuous social restraints with which Sterne has confronted him, Tristram Shandy must tell the story of his sexual misfortunes: he must do so because these misfortunes have determined his life, and his life is his primary topic. It is by developing the conflict which thus arises between Tristram and society that Sterne has achieved his satire of social hypocrisy. To understand it, we must first understand how and how far Tristram has been able to carry on his story.

I Tristram's Equivocal Testimony

We may introduce ourselves to Tristram's devices by considering this little passage in which he has presented Toby and Walter discussing Mrs. Shandy's choice of the midwife instead of Dr. Slop as the attendant to her delivery: "'My sister, mayhap,' quoth my uncle *Toby*, 'does not choose to let a man come so near her****.' Make this dash,—'tis an Aposiopesis.—Take the dash away, and write *Backside*,—'tis Bawdy.—Scratch Backside out, and put *Cover'd-way* in,—'tis a Metaphor" (100). If we notice here that Tristram has not written "Backside" except as an unsatisfactory solution to his communicative problem, we will have hit on one of his two major stylistic devices for publishing his story's obscenity: this is his sterile didactic tone toward his story, his sense of it not as an affective thing in itself, but as a vehicle for public edification. If we notice, on the other hand, that the expression "scratch Backside" (instead, say, of "erase Backside") may draw Madam's and Sir's minds beyond the term to what the term stands for, we will have approached Tristram's second major device: this is his equivocal extension—his suggesting or, at least, allowing a second meaning or value to his words besides their primary, explicit one.

Tristram's Trial by Prudery

By taking up, first, Tristram's scholarly sterilization of his story and, second, his equivocal extension of it, we will come to see how he has made his hypocritical audience attend to so extensive and so pointed a sexual report as he had to give them.

Tristram, first of all then, sterilizes many admittedly obscene elements in his life story by considering them as scholarly and didactic items, rather than as emotionally evocative ones. By maintaining his scholarly detachment, an attitude which we have already observed, Tristram has been able to cover his life's obscenities as with a garment (637) and to treat them with extensive if clinical particularity. Owing in large part to this attitude, he has been able to consider such topics as his parents' copulation (434-39;4-9), the elasticity of his mother's womb (149-54), and the stages of his own birth—all without giving his audience real offence or embarrassment.

One element in this sterilization is Tristram's extensive use of scholarly jargon and research. He has often clothed obscene items in such terms as *"Argumentum Tripodium," "Argumentum ad Rem"* (71), and *"a posteriori"* (597) from the language of rhetoric, and such as *"phimosis"* (401), "evacuations," "repletions," *"non-naturals"* (76), *"os pubis,"* and *"coxendix"* (79) from that of medicine. Tristram has carefully abstracted an expression, *"petite canulle,"* from a learned French paper on pre-birth baptism (62) and used it in offering a refinement on the French proposal.

Extended quotation of scholarly sources has often been required to endow a subject with a sufficiently sterile air. Tristram has thus purified for public scrutiny the topic of his mother's lying in (99ff) and his incendiary discussions of noses (215ff) and whiskers (343-48). His use of scholarship in sterilizing his explanation of the fifty different ends for which a woman might choose a man as a husband, a necessary part of his account of Uncle Toby's amours, is especially dextrous:

> The imagery under which *Slawkenbergius* impresses this upon his reader's fancy, in the beginning of his third Decad, is so ludicrous, that the honour I bear the sex, will not suffer me to quote it—otherwise 'tis not destitute of humour.
>
> "She first, saith *Slawkenbergius,* stops the asse, and holding his halter in her left hand (lest he should get away) she thrusts her right hand into the very bottom of his pannier to search for it—For what?—

you'll not know the sooner, quoth *Slawkenbergius,* for interrupting me—

"I have nothing, good Lady, but empty bottles," says the asse.

"I'm loaded with tripes," says the second.

—And thou art little better, quoth she to the third; for nothing is there in thy panniers but trunk-hose and pantofles—and so to the fourth and fifth, going on one by one through the whole string, till coming to the asse which carries it, she turns the pannier upside down, looks at it—considers it—samples it—measures it—stretches it—wets it —dries it—then takes her teeth both to the warp and weft of it—

—Of what? for the love of Christ!

I am determined, answered *Slawkenbergius,* that all the powers upon earth shall never wring that secret from my breast.   (624-25)

Tristram has clothed his conclusion to the dangerously suggestive Whiskers interlude (347-48) in the same kind of scholarly dress, making the curate d'Estella responsible for the equivocal definition of the term "whiskers."

Tristram has reinforced his own use of scholarship with generous infusions of Walter's, suggesting some of the dangers his head was to suffer in birth, for example, by rehearsing Walter's study and reasoning on the matter (144-45). He has also cooled off the topic of noses, an essential element to our understanding of his unlucky birth, by developing it in the form of an annotated bibliography of Walter's library of noses (224-34). There were Bruscambille's prologue on long noses and Erasmus on their application; there were the disputations of Ambrose Paræus, Prignitz, and Scroderus; and there was, lastly, the great folio of long noses by Slawkenbergius, which superseded all the others. By developing Walter's close pursuit of this topic, especially his editorial attack on the phrase *"ad excitandum focum"* (229-30), Tristram has led his audience right up to the most unmentionable of topics. His reference to Walter's studies of Gothic antiquity (434-35) and of *Spencer de Legibus Hebræorum Ritualibus* (384-87), again, has helped Tristram sterilize his account of his window-sash misfortune and its aftereffects.

Walter Shandy was often more concerned with his studies than with his life, putting a hypothesis, for instance, ahead of his family's good name (68-69). But Tristram's scholarly attention is focussed, quite properly, on the materials of his life. Indeed, Tris-

tram is often high-handed with secondary sources: he is sometimes too hurried to consult or check them (24;63); he sometimes
becomes impatient with their jargon (40) and skeptical of their
truth (53). Before he has finished his book, he throws away the
key to his study (342-43) and is later forced to improvise his research (456-57). But, in the handling of his life, Tristram is extremely careful and precise; he devotes himself to getting its
events and their connections exactly right and to drawing from
them the general truths they contain. He has thus been able to
give a vastly particular report on all his life's vital elements from
the hard problem of his begettings' exact date through Uncle
Toby's amours, that complete system of love and love-making, by
treating every element of it in this sterile scholarly way.

His scholarly attitude, however, for all its purity, has obviously
not allowed Tristram to give society a complete and exact report
of his life. To extend the report he has given, to shadow forth admissions and complaints no gentleman could explicitly publicize,
Tristram has resorted to the dangerous device of equivocation.
He has halved his story with his audience as he planned and
promised to do, leaving them some things to imagine for themselves. Sometimes this halving has been mere courtesy, as when
Tristram furnished a blank page for each gentleman to draw his
own idea of the widow Wadman (470-71) and when he set aside
a black page for all his readers' mourning of Yorick (34-34). But
usually Tristram has so calculated, so grooved these equivocal
openings as to lead his audience powerfully if darkly toward
dreadful and embarrassing conclusions. We must now see how he
has done this.

Some critics have made much of Tristram's choice of words,[1] perhaps remembering his assertion that Uncle Toby's "life was put in
jeopardy by words" (87). And, indeed, much can be learned from
a study of Tristram's equivocal vocabulary. But this study will
chiefly show that it is not really Tristram's words but the uses he
has put them to, the contexts in which he has submerged them,
that have given them their power to extend the fancies of his audience. Tristram has not actually attributed the power over
Toby's life to words, anyway: the statement to that effect was
chiefly a rhetorical flourish. It is really "the unsteady uses of
words," as Tristram said a bit earlier, which perplexed Toby

and which have, indeed, "perplexed the clearest and most exalted understandings" (86).

A nice proof that his own unsteady uses are Tristram's chief means of equivocating his discourse and perplexing his audience with unmentionable fancies is furnished by his great reliance on vague, general terms to achieve his equivocal effects. Such empty expressions as "means" (473), "matters" (434), "affairs" (66), "kinds of bodies" (453), and "a certain wind instrument" (75) are native to Tristram's equivocal art. Their chief value for Tristram, quite clearly, is their responsiveness to his unsteady uses. "It" and "thing" which can be bent into any shapes at all, are, as we will see, Tristram's favorite words. Take, however, as a first example, his handling of the vague term "means." Tristram has narrowed it down to a couple of meanings by reporting his father as saying to his mother that Toby "may as well batter away his means upon that [his marriage to Mrs. Wadman] as anything else." Walter has used the empty word "one" in his letter of amatory advice to Toby in such a way that it can refer either to Mrs. Wadman or to the devil (591). Tristram, again, has treated the general term "faculties" (13) by telling us that Didius, who had invented a phrase he wanted to add to the licenses of midwives, "coax'd many of the old licens'd matrons to open their faculties afresh, in order to have this whim-wham of his inserted."

The vaguer and more general a word is, the more useful it is to Sterne's equivocater. Tristram has used the term "part," for instance, in extending our perceptions of both male and female beyond what society allows. A hot chestnut drew "Phutatorius's attention toward the part" (321); and Toby, again, can have "the part annointed with hellebore" if love keeps plaguing him (572). On the other hand, Toby's assertion that there was no harm in the Roman prætor Gallus's lying with his own wife caught hold of a woman, Mrs. Shandy, "by the weak part of the whole sex" (367-68) —meaning, Tristram has assured Madam, her curiosity. Then again, he tells us that Walter wished to preserve the Shandy family custom "that the eldest son of it should have free ingress, egress, and regress into foreign parts before marriage,—not only for the sake of bettering his own private parts, by the benefit of exercise and change of so much air—but simply for the mere delectation of his fancy, by the feather put into his cap, of having been abroad" (333). Here the term has been equivocated so as to extend our imagination first of one sex and then of the other; and yet the term is so subtly set in the flow of this long easy sentence that many readers, both male and female, may pass by with out noticing a thing.

More useful to Tristram even than "part" are the still vaguer terms "thing" and "it." This passage should make clear their malleableness and thus their wonderful sensitivity to Tristram's equivocal style: "I have but half a score things to do in the time— I have a thing to name—a thing to lament—a thing to hope—a thing to promise, and a thing to threaten—I have a thing to suppose—a thing to declare—a thing to conceal—a thing to chuse, and a thing to pray for.—This chapter, therefore, I *name* the chapter of THINGS—and my next chapter to it, that is, the first chapter of my next volume, if I live, shall be my chapter upon WHISKERS, in order to keep up some sort of connection in my works" (336-37). Tristram has found many uses for this term and its variations, "something" and "nothing" (83;158;49;185;376), as in this passage from the introduction to Uncle Toby's hobbyhorse, for instance:

Never did lover post down to a belov'd mistress with more heat and expectation, than my uncle *Toby* did, to enjoy this self-same thing [his bowling green] in private;—I say in private;—for it was sheltered from a house, as I told you, by a tall yew hedge, and was covered on the other three sides, from mortal sight, by rough holly and thickset flowering shrubs;—so that the idea of not being seen, did not a little contribute to the idea of pleasure pre-conceived in my uncle *Toby's* mind. —Vain thought! however thick it was planted about,—or private soever it might seem,—to think, dear uncle *Toby*, of enjoying a thing which took up a whole rood and a half of ground,—and not have it known! (98-99)

"Thing" can stand for "bowling green" well enough; but the emphasis on 'its' secrecy and on 'its' being planted thickly about suggest a second idea as well. If we put this equivocal use of "thing" with another similar one on Toby's "something," we may get an idea of how Tristram fills out his story with his equivocations: ". . . in following my uncle *Toby's* forefinger with hers [Mrs. Wadman's], close thro' all the little turns and indentings of

his works—pressing sometimes against the side of it—then treading upon it's nail—then tripping it up—then touching it here—
then there, and so on—it set something at least in motion" (555).
These two equivocal passages, especially when taken with another of like import on Toby's "centre" (554-56), should give the
necessary weight to Tristram's statement, late in the novel
(626), that Toby was sexually potent despite his wound and despite what the world may have thought or said.

Tristram has found the pronominal "it" even more useful than
"thing" in shadowing forth the unmentionable mysteries of his
story (608;401;343;550-51;160;624;572). "It" can be used in the
most abrupt equivocation, such as the "out upon it" with which
Tristram has responded to the ripping of his breeches (524); or
it can be carried on and on, repeated quite naturally and easily,
as it has been in Tristram's explanation of the fifty different ends
for which a woman may choose a husband (624-25), a passage already quoted in this chapter. Often, as in the continuation of that
passage, Tristram has involved both "it" and "thing" in his equivocations. We find cases of this in the passage which interrupts the
assertion "It is with love as with CUCKOLDOM" (540) and in this
one from the dedication of Book IX to a great man: "Having, *a
priori,* intended to dedicate *The Amours of my uncle Toby* to Mr.
***—I see more reasons, *a posteriori,* for doing it to
Lord*******. [¶] I should lament from my soul, if this exposed
me to the jealousy of their Reverences; because, *a posteriori,* in
Court-latin signifies, the kissing hands for preferment—or anything else—in order to get it" (597). Here "thing" is equivocal: it
may be parallel to "hands," being something else that is kissed, or,
as seems more likely at first, to "preferment," being something else
that is gotten by kissing hands. However, the "it," being singular,
must refer to "preferment" and that tilts "thing" to the first alternative. At the same time it infects *"a posteriori"* with a comple-
mentary meaning and makes the whole passage verge on an unspeakable indictment of courtiers and politicians.

Tristram has, of course, achieved equivocal textures sometimes
by using ready-made equivocal terms. He has used some tradi-
tional cant terms such as "horn works" (110-11), "green gowns,"
and "old hats" (363); and he has traded on suggestive names such
as Kunastrokius (13), Phutatorius (318), Scroderus (234), and

[72]

Slawkenbergius (230), which we may think of as ready-made (by Sterne) for him. But Tristram's two most infamous equivocal terms, "nose" (215ff) and "whiskers" (343-48), and most minor ones, such as "spouts" (382), "stump" (628), "trench" (583), "breeches" (609), "furred cap" (549), and "pie" (551), owe their equivocal force, like his vague, general terms, to Tristram's un-steady uses. It is from their entanglements in his story and his dis-course that these commonly denotative terms have come to draw the minds of Madam and Sir toward unmentionable ideas.

These cant and canted terms, moreover, are not really verbal in their suggestive power, as a pun is, but figurative. Tristram is thus a dealer in what Joseph Addison defined as true wit, that is, in resemblances between things, rather than in false wit, that is, in resemblances between words.[2] Tristram did not abhor the false wit of puns as his father did (111), but puns are, nevertheless, rather rare in his conversation. Such words as "shift" (412), with its two totally different meanings (1. an expedient; 2. an undergar-ment), did not usually suit his needs. Tristram has worked, rather, with words whose one clearly denoted object—such as a spout, a hat, or a nose—resembles some other object: "—Fair and softly, gentle reader!—where is thy fancy carrying thee?—if there is truth in man, by my great grandfather's nose, I mean the external organ of smelling, or that part of man which stands prominent in his face,—and which painters say, in good jolly noses and well-proportioned faces, should comprehend a full third,—that is, measuring downwards from the setting on of the hair.—[¶]—What a life of it has an author, at this pass!" (221). It is not the word "nose" that extends our thoughts; it is the likeness which Tristram has made us recognize of a nose to some other thing which may also comprehend a full third measuring downwards from the setting on of the hair. Tristram never sets tall opaque words between his reader and his meaning; what he sets rather are images which may, when unsteadily handled, lead the reader to entertain in his fancy other resembling images. All the cant terms Tristram has taken from tradition and all he has himself canted have this figurative rather than a verbal equivocalness.

Often Tristram's equivocal practice has been explicitly figura-tive, as in his account of Mrs. Wadman's sentry-box maneuvers (554-56). Tristram has concluded that episode, ". . . my uncle

Toby being thus attacked and sore push'd on both his wings—was it a wonder, if now and then, it put his centre into disorder?" This is an appropriate military metaphor: Tristram is clearly likening Toby's leg and forefingers, whose part in the action has just been described, to the two wings of an army; but what is Tristram likening to the army's center? Often the metaphorical extension is subtler than this. What caused Yorick to give up his expenditure on fine horses, Tristram tells us, "was this, that it confined all his charity into one particular channel, and where, as he fancied, it was the least wanted, namely, to the child-bearing and child-getting part of the parish; preserving nothing for the impotent . . ." (21). The word "channel," although obviously figurative, need not be closely interpreted; but its use in this context, especially since it has been followed up by the distinction between the fertile and the sterile, suggests one certain imaginative extension. If Madam is dull, she will miss it, however, just as she will miss this next figure which has been complicated by its dependence on gesture: "The laws of nature," said Walter Shandy, "will defend themselves;—but error—(he would add, looking earnestly at my mother)—error, Sir, creeps in thro' the minute holes, and small crevices, which human nature leaves unguarded" (146). Madam may imagine that a wall is the structure Walter has in mind here, but a passage which has come before (101-02) and one which will follow (218) might lead her to imagine some other structure.

We might notice in closing this sketch of Tristram's equivocal vocabulary that his vague terms and his figurative terms overlap. Tristram's treatment of such vague expressions as "instrument" (75) and "faculties" (13) allows his readers different sets of images. And imagistic words like "spouts" and "channels" and "crevices" owe their multiple possibilities of meaning to their generality: there are several kinds of structures, for instance, in which we might find a crevice; and there are several kinds of crevices. In both cases, it is Tristram's unsteady uses, his contextual contrivances, that lead the private fancies of his audience beyond a decorous meaning to an unmentionable one.

We must now try to sketch in Tristram's equivocal contexts, his artfully unsteady uses. In passing, we may notice that modifiers are often important—as in this statement: "No ideas are so totally different as those of Ministers, and innocent lovers" (597-98). Here "innocent" casts a bad light back on the unmodified "Ministers," suggesting that ministers are not innocent. However, it is not modification, but placing that gives Tristram's equivocations their special quality; and the essence of his placing is suspense. By suspending significant matter, for a phrase or a dozen pages, Tristram has given the substantive terms and the modifications out of which he has formed his discourse their powerful suggestive aura.

We may, for convenience, define all his suspensions into two kinds: these are the hold-off and the false-lead. The hold-off is an apparently empty and innocent suspension which is concluded by a suggestion that stains it. The false-lead is the opposite of this: it is a suggestive suspension which is concluded by a contradiction of the suggestion. The false-lead is more useful since it is continually suggestive and can thus be infinitely drawn out; it is also more insidious since, at its close, the prudish reader may find himself entertaining bawdy notions of which Tristram has just shown himself to be free.

Of course, our definition of any single suspension depends partly on our sense of Tristram's intentions, which are never certain, and partly on our sense of Madam's and Sir's imaginations, which they have curtained with impenetrable decency. Tristram, although we have evidence of his vast and brilliant self-consciousness, may simply have been careless at this or that moment of his discourse: it is only his discourse that we have and not his open mind. Madam and Sir, again, may be dull or pure, in which case they will miss the most suggestive false-lead entirely; or they may be hypersensitive, as Tristram has sometimes complained (217-18;221;49), and thus find every hold-off, even those that end in innocence, to be a texture of unspeakable hints and shadows. One charm of this book is just this: its different value for a reader each time he reads it, the shifting of its equivocal penumbra as one's own mind quickens, slows down or otherwise varies. With these reservations, however, we may still cover Tristram's equivocal suspensions well enough under the heads of hold-off and false-lead.

Many hold-offs are virtually harmless, mere continuations of Tristram's conversational, suspensive style, as in this example:

[75]

"What these perplexities of my uncle Toby were,—'tis impossible you should guess;—if you could,—I should blush; not as a relation,—not as a man,—not even as a woman,—but I should blush as an author" (80). The hold-offs of Susannah's simile (287), and of the explanation of Toby's blush (97) are similarly innocent though even these may tickle itchy imaginations. But it never hurts for Madam to be alert, for the most innocent hold-off may be loaded: "—I won't go about to argue the point with you,—'tis so,—and I am persuaded of it, madam, as much as can be; 'That both men and women bear pain or sorrow, (and, for aught I know, pleasure too) best in a horizontal position'" (215). We might notice Tristram's use of the vague terms "it" and "point" in keeping this suspension empty. Such terms have also allowed Tristram to work the *a posteriori* hold-off quoted just above. Such innocent, empty suspensions could not have been carried on very long without ruining the equivocal quality of Tristram's discourse: these we have discussed are typical. However, Tristram has managed a somewhat longer one in giving his father's reasons for warmer climates' producing greater geniuses: with such terms as "faculties," "affairs," and "fairest parts," he keeps his audience for half a page in the belief that Walter's reasoning is focussed on fine heads instead of on flexible wombs (151-52). Trim's waving of his stick, which Tristram takes at its close not as an example of liberty, as the reader expected, but more precisely as an example of celibacy (603-04), is another more extended hold-off. But none of them has been carried very far. In every case, a brief uncertainty is concluded with a bawdy hint.

The false-lead is a more versatile device. It can be as short as this: "My mother—madam—was so [that is, lewd] at no time" (600); or as long as Tristram's discussion of noses (214ff) which he finally abandoned (273) without ever having been able to reverse its bawdy suggestiveness. A false-lead's reversal, as these two cases suggest, may be complete or highly qualified. There are exact contradictions: "—But for my father's ass—oh! mount him —mount him—mount him—(that's three times, is it not?) mount him not" (584). There are others, such as Yorick's explanation of his satisfaction with his slow, feeble horse, whose suggestions and reversals form merely a ripple in Tristram's conversation. Yorick would explain that while moseying along at his mount's natural gait "he could draw up an argument in his sermon,—or a hole in his breeches . . . he could unite and reconcile everything,—he could compose his sermon,—he could compose his cough,—and, in case nature gave a call that way, he could likewise compose himself to sleep" (20). Those readers who allow their imaginations to take a low road at 'nature's call' are soon deserted by the innocent Tristram, but many readers will never see a crossroads at all.

Seemingly complete reversals, like Susannah's exclamation over the mutilated Tristram (376), may be less decisive than they seem. "Nothing is left—for me" may really indicate the same loss as "Nothing is left"; and so may "Nothing is left—for me, but to run my country," since only a major mishap could cause so long a flight. The green gowns false-lead (363), although complete in its contradiction, is subtle in style:

Stay—I have a small account to settle with the reader, before *Trim* can go on with his harangue.—It shall be done in two minutes.

Amongst many other book-debts, all of which I shall discharge in due time,—I own myself a debtor to the world for two items,—a chapter upon *chamber-maids* and *button-holes*, which, in the former part of my work, I promised and fully intended to pay off this year: but some of your worships and reverences telling me, that the two subjects, especially so connected together, might endanger the morals of the world,—I pray the chapter upon chamber-maids and button-holes may be forgiven me,—and that they will accept of the last chapter in lieu of it; which is nothing, an't please your reverences, but a chapter of *chamber-maids, green-gowns,* and *old hats.*

Trim took his off the ground,—put it upon his head,—and then went on with his oration upon death, in manner and form following. (363)

Here Tristram has picked up a bawdy false-lead, one he introduced and suspended some pages back (289-90;337). It depends on Your Worships' and Reverences' recognizing cant values in the key terms; and Tristram, by his self-conscious bunching and substitution, has made this recognition almost certain. However, immediately after uttering the terms, he implicitly denies that he himself has made this recognition: by "old hat" Tristram has always meant such a head-piece as Trim's and thus by "green gowns" only such garments as those which Susannah hoped to get from Bobby Shandy's death. Tristram has made an equally graceful escape from the outrageous implications of his "furred cap" foolery:

—"Not touch it for the world" did I say—
Lord, how I have heated my imagination with this metaphor!

CHAP. XIII.

Which shews, let your reverences and worships say what you will of it (for as for *thinking*—all who *do* think—think pretty much alike, both upon it and other matters)—LOVE is certainly, at least alphabetically speaking, one of the most
Agitating [etc.].   (551)

Here Tristram has used "it" to ease his discourse from the incendiary "furred cap" to the cooler and more general "love."

Often we find a mingling of the qualities of the hold-off and the false-lead. Walter Shandy's two beds of justice (434-39), for instance, is a whole series of false-leads—"He is growing a very tall lad. . . . He is very tall for his age. . . . I cannot conceive. . . . I am very short myself" and so on—which ends in a piece of information, that "this was on *Sunday* night," which makes the whole thing, at least for a hitherto unsuspecting reader, a hold-off, giving a sudden bawdy turn to seemingly innocent matter. The extensive narrative suspense of Toby's modesty (67ff) also partakes of both qualities, as does Tristram's wonderfully involved suspension of the "it" which Toby resolved to show to Mrs. Wadman and which she resolved to see (623ff). The explanation of Toby's thoughts will reveal this as a false-lead; that of the widow's as a hold-off. Tristram's handling of Dr. Slop's drawing of his****** from his green baize bag (184-86) gives us an especially fine suspensive texture. He has, first of all, held off his story to discuss this ****** (six letters, please note). And he starts his discussion simply by holding off the mystery term with "it" and "thing." Then with "BAMBINO," as an example of what ancient orators could hide under their mantles (as Slop has hid his ****** in the green baize bag), he gives us a false lead; and, with the "nothing . . . Madam, worth showing" that modern orators can hide under their less flowing attire, he gives another. But this is not all. The forceps (seven letters) that Slop meant to produce to clinch his argument with Toby turns out to be still another false lead, one which is finally resolved as Tristram returns to his story and explains what Slop actually brought forth—the forceps gripping a squirt (six letters at last).

Despite his great skill in sterilizing his life story and in extending it with equivocation, Tristram has obviously been unable to declare its facts exactly. We do not know the nature of his misfortune at birth nor the extent of his window-sash mutilation: we do not know whether his vigor has been impaired or merely his figure in the world. But, by sterilizing his life's vital events, Tristram has been able to report them; and by equivocating their final results, he has been able to suggest, if not to assert, their crucial importance. He has thus presented society with the decisive actions in his life and surrounded their telling with that halo of impotence which is, whether true or false, profoundly relevant to the communication he has been working to achieve—that he is desolate and that his family is doomed.

II *Sterne's Satiric Accusation*

To understand the satiric relevance of Tristram's sterilized and equivocated presentation of his life, we must see that it allows, throughout its course, two profoundly different visions of sex: first, we have the conventionally bawdy view which is fostered by society's prudery; and, second, a truer, broader view which arises naturally from Tristram's story. We must define this second view of sex before going on.

Sex was not for Tristram a brief, unmentionable diversion, a mere topic for bawdy fooling—not really; it was, rather, a vital, in his case, disastrous human act. Sex, as his story reveals it, is triangular, familial: it is, to use Walter Shandy's words, "the conjunction betwixt male and female for the procreation of the species" (390). Tristram's comic handling of his story has brought out the comic side of this vision of sex: its humor arises from the helplessness of those involved in the act of sexual begetting and from the act's outlandish consequences.

The humor of the begetters' helplessness comes chiefly from Walter Shandy's paternal efforts and defeats. Walter tried to influence Tristram's conception with a careful concentration of his physical and mental powers (296), to assure his being born whole by bringing in Dr. Slop to attend the birth, and to name him

Trismegistus. There are several humorous aspects to the defeats
Walter suffered in these paternal struggles—the odd objects of his
concern; his scholarly mode of action; his dependence on such unlikely auxiliaries as Dr. Slop, Susannah, and, of course, Mrs.
Shandy. But not all of these are really absurd. A cerebellum and
a "nose," take "nose" either way or both ways, do matter; and how
might a father carry out plans to protect his emergent child, if
plans he has, other than through an obstetrician? It is in having
plans at all that Walter is chiefly absurd. With all his study
(because of it?), he has failed to understand and take, as the
thoughtless Mrs. Shandy did, a true and natural part in his child's
beginnings. Once the brief and chancy act of begetting is behind
them, parents have, Tristram's story suggests, no other useful
business than to hope for the best and prepare for the worst.

The consequences of begetting are humorous in their falling
on the third—the inactive and merely potential—member of the
sexual triangle, and in the disproportion between their life-long
extent and the brief act from which they follow. Sterne has given
an ironical emphasis to the actual focus of the consequences by
having the real sufferer, Tristram, seem completely detached and
unconcerned. He describes his unscathed father in one paternal
agony after another, while himself maintaining almost perfect
composure. He does briefly 'sympathize' with Walter over the
mashing of his nose (215) and over his misnaming (55-56); but it
was really on Walter, Tristram seems to feel, that these calamities
fell (292). Sterne brings out the absurd disproportion between
the sexual act and its procreative consequences by keeping up his
hero's double presence as the pre-infant and infant sufferer of
some trivial accidents, and as the incurably odd and unlucky gentleman these accidents have produced. From the adult Tristram's
voluminous if unemotional attention to his own conception and
birth we may infer that the sexual union of real consequence to
him—and is the same not true of any man?—is that by which he
was begotten. *Ecce homunculus: ecce homo.*

One is not sure how the members of society may understand
the sexual references which accompany Tristram's account of his
unfortunate beginnings; but, in fact, they almost all carry its procreative and familial vision of sex. Those related directly to Tristram's story—such as the Shandy marriage articles, the argu-

ment over the midwife, Walter Shandy's suggestion that his wife deliver their child through a Caesarian section, and Dr. Slop's obstetric equipment—naturally carry it. And many digressive pieces, like Tristram's odd bit on pre-birth baptism, do too. He has quoted the opinion of the learned French council, that it is permissible to baptise an unemerged child provided the thing can be done *"par le moyen d'une petite canulle"* and *"sans faire aucun tort a la mere";* and then he has proposed a refinement on their plan, that all the children of a marriage be pre-baptised at once, after the wedding and before consummation, "provided . . . the thing can be done . . . *par le moyen d'une* petite canulle, and *sans faire aucun tort au pere"* (58-62). Sterne also recalls sexual procreation in the explanation of how Yorick had confined "all his charity into one particular channel . . . namely . . . the child-bearing and child-getting part of his parish" (21). And the "nothing" in Tristram's admission that under their short coats modern orators "can conceal nothing . . . Madam, worth showing," may recall "BAMBINO" as well as something else: a baby has been Tristram's illustration of what ancient orators could hide, until the right moment, under their mantles. (185-86).

All the sexual allusions in the account of Tristram's beginnings, whether they admit procreation or not, are woven into its richly familial texture. The discussion of short coats and mantles, for instance, helps explain Dr. Slop's dramatic production of his forceps whose relation to the emerging Tristram is clear enough. Tristram's suggestion that pleasure as well as pain might best be borne in a horizontal position introduces Walter Shandy in his prone attitude of deep paternal distress. And, although there is no chance of offspring in Phutatorius's sexual pleasure and pain, the meeting at which Phutatorius suffers eventually gets down to the question of a mother's kinship to her own child. The sexual allusions after Tristram has turned to Uncle Toby's amours (422ff), of course, lack this interweaving in a narrative design dedicated to Sterne's broad understanding of sex. Moreover, the allusions themselves seldom stress procreation: there is little sign of it in Trim's amour with the beguine (568-75), in the story of his brother's courtship of the sausage seller's widow (603-09), or in Tristram's own "furred cap" foolery (549-51); and there is none at all in the story of the abbess of Andoüillets (503-10). However,

Tristram's continued concern with his father and his Uncle Toby should serve society as a constant reminder of sex's vast personal consequences and its family ties.

Society, however, has the option of taking these late pages of Tristram's discourse and, indeed, virtually every reference he has made to sex, merely for the bawdry in it. The early piece on pre-birth baptism, for instance, may lead Madam and Sir merely to worry about the insertion in mothers' wombs of the "petite canulle." Tristram's explanation of Dr. Slop's rhetorical production of his forceps, again, allows them to replace the bambino ancient orators hid under their mantles with another secret object; and they may take Walter's two beds of justice only as a titillating bit of foolery. Even Tristram's account of his begetting, with Sir's question and Tristram's quibble, may cause ladies and gentlemen to murmur: "The idea of their own son's revealing the Shandys' arrangements!"

This, then, is the satiric value of Tristram's pointed but equivocal presentation of sex: it allows the members of society to take the high sexual road or the low—to see sex in its true human proportion or to see it as merely an unmentionable diversion. Almost every time one of them—one of us—finds mere bawdry in Tristram's life story, he is implicating himself in society's sexual hypocrisy. He has let society's prudery warp his mind so that he ignores the true relevance of sex in Tristram's life—in all human life—and exalts the mere activity of lust.

This satiric definition of social hypocrisy and of hypocrisy's effect on its members, although it radiates brilliantly from Sterne's novel, is essentially implicit, undeclared. Tristram can never openly accuse Madam or Sir of sexual hypocrisy or of sexual astigmatism: they never really give themselves away—whatever Sterne's audience may have done. Madam has almost revealed herself a number of times. "Fy! Mr. *Shandy*," she once exclaimed—in what tone of voice we cannot be sure—when Tristram was rehearsing the possible ties binding Jenny and himself (49). Madam seems to approach a damaging admission more closely still in twice asking whether "the stranger's nose was a true nose" (272) and with her extreme curiosity over the tests a woman makes when she is considering a man for a husband (625). But Madam, like Sir, remains blank and grave—respectable to the last. The Victorians,[3] who have taken up Madam's and Sir's parts, have not, however, been so discreet. A brief glance at any of their attacks on Tristram's bawdiness—attacks which actually confess their own—will show how powerfully Tristram's equivocations have worked on Sterne's hypocritical readers.

Sterne has not left his satire of social hypocrisy and its individual effects entirely to implication, however. He has focussed it, toward his novel's close, by giving us one fully developed example: the widow Wadman. Because of her fear of the world's regard, because of her social circumspection, Mrs. Wadman so tangled and involved the question of Toby's potency as to make it insoluble. If she could have asked Toby straight out whether he was sexually potent or not, he would have told her, just as he revealed his love for her to Corporal Trim (580) and to the widow herself (633), just as he explained the state of his riding blister to the company at Shandy Hall (585). Indeed, had the widow's unadmitted concern for Toby's potency not blinded her to Toby himself, she might have found assurance in his declaration of love and in his proposal of marriage. Toby's explanation to Walter and Yorick of his feeling for Mrs. Wadman, as one which would "make a man marry, and love his wife, and get a few children," showed, as Yorick said, that Toby understood marriage quite well enough (585-87); and he would not have volunteered for its duties, honest soldier that he was, if he had been unable to perform any of them.

It is important that we understand the final assurance Sterne has given us that Toby was sexually potent. He strongly implied it with the equivocal description of Mrs. Wadman's effect on Toby's "something" and on his "centre" and with Toby's statement on marriage. And Tristram has put it out of doubt in this assertion:

. . . with regard to my uncle *Toby's* fitness for the marriage state, nothing was ever better: she [nature] had formed him of the best and kindliest clay—had temper'd it with her own milk, and breathed into it the sweetest spirit—she had made him all gentle, generous and humane—she had fill'd his heart with trust and confidence, and disposed

every passage which led to it, for the communication of the tenderest
offices—she had moreover considered the other causes for which matri-
money was ordained—

And accordingly ✻
✻ ✻
✻ .

The DONATION was not defeated by my uncle *Toby's* wound.
(626)[4]

Everything personal, then, was conducive to their marriage, as
Walter Shandy said (589); everything, in fact, except for the
doubts and the restraints imposed on Mrs. Wadman by the gossip-
ing and the censoriousness of society. She was the most mar-
riageable creature in the feminine world, a daughter of Eve
(546); and Toby was potentially the world's most perfect husband
and father. But that tyranny of society, which Walter predicted
would put off their wedding for a year (589), ruined it forever.

Social gossip plagued the widow with a doubt of Toby which
social decorum would not allow her to resolve. Driven by this
dilemma, she used her interest in Toby's profession, her concern
for his health, and even the subject of children all to discover his
potency without seeming to have asked. Her monomania caused
her to turn all of Toby's wonderful matrimonial virtues, in Tristram's phrase, "into nothing but *empty bottles, tripes, trunk-hose,*
and *pantofles*" (626). She abused humanity, that comprehensive
virtue for which Toby was prepared to praise her (624), and
turned it into lust, just as Walter Shandy said (644).

Tristram suggests a similarity between Mrs. Wadman and the
ladies in his audience when he allows each gentleman present to
draw the widow's portrait after his own mistress (470-71). But
Sterne has not insisted on the similarity. Indeed, Sterne never insists on his readers' sexual hypocrisy nor on their hypocritical
exaltation of mere lust. He might well have expected them, even
the hypocritical ones, to see something of sex's broader importance in human life since he had revealed it to them in Tristram
Shandy's conception, birth, and family devotion with such particularity and precision.

CHAPTER 6

The Reader Shall Decide

IT was for the sake of its social reception, as we have seen, that Tristram labored to make his life story instructive, amusing, and decent. He lusted earnestly and endeavored carefully so that Madam and Sir would find everything that had touched him interesting and lively. He was especially careful to enlist their attention and interest at his story's most odd, painful, and obscene moments. Thus the interpretation of Tristram's life story has been sharply focussed on this representative society which is Tristram's audience and, by obvious extension, on the actual members of society who are its readers.

If we look back over Tristram's efforts to expand his life's peculiarity (Chapter 3) and to transform its tragedy (Chapter 4), we will see, moreover, that every element of Tristram's story— and not merely its obscenity—is subject to its readers' interpretation. Tristram's creator, by making sex a major ingredient of his life, has made sex a sort of objective correlative of Tristram's whole discursive problem and of his audience's whole interpretive problem. But Tristram's social adjustment of his life's obscenity (Chapter 5) is merely a part of his vast problem of adjusting for social scrutiny all the crucial elements of his life from before birth to death. It is thus Tristram's whole life, finally, that Sterne's readers must interpret and judge.

Tristram has allowed his audience interpretive options over his life's many odd, non-sexual items similar to those we saw him leave them over its obscenity. He sterilizes, for instance, the long swearing episode that took place in Shandy Hall on his birthday. By using the same scientific and didactic detachment with which he clothed his conception and birth, Tristram has been able to give society, without any offense, the world's most absolute curse as well as several others of lesser note (164-84). He has employed a false-lead to suggest an unfilial judgment on his father's *Tristrapædia:* "—No,—I think I have advanced nothing, replied my father, making answer to a question which *Yorick* had taken the liberty to put to him,—I have advanced nothing in the *Tristrapædia,* but what is as clear as any one proposition in *Euclid*" (389). Simply by interrupting Walter's statement in his usual easy way and then taking it up again with a little natural repetition, Tristram has shaded the word "nothing" with a meaning Walter never intended and has thus hinted at a feeling for Walter's peculiar treatise which no dutiful son could state publicly. Tristram's audience is free, of course, to recognize this feeling or not.

Tristram has had to give the same sort of ambiguous rendering to all his direct admissions of his life's tragedies. He admits his imminent death, for instance, in his tender apostrophe to Jenny but then destroys its effect with this impudent flirt at his audience: "Now, for what the world thinks of that ejaculation—I would not give a groat" (611). He similarly reverses the damaging admission that "my OPINIONS will be the death of me" by turning his attention, first, to the effect these voluminous opinions may have on Your Worships' eyes and, second, to their effect on the dwindling supply of paper and geese (285-86). Tristram has led society toward and then from an admission of his impending death more pointedly still in this late equivocation: "To this hour art thou not tormented with the vile asthma thou gattest in skating against the wind in *Flanders?* and is it but two months ago, that in a fit of laughter, on seeing a cardinal make water like a quirister (with both hands) thou brakest a vessel in thy lungs, whereby, in two hours, thou lost as many quarts of blood; and hadst thou lost as much more, did not the faculty tell thee—it would have amounted to a gallon?" (545). This reversal is what has been called a false-lead; but the consequence which Tristram has dodged, that a second such loss of blood would have been fatal, is clearly not false: it is merely too personal and too painful for direct social utterance. This passage has been sterilized, we may notice, as well as equivocated—with the reference to the faculty and with an item from their arithmetical wisdom. As we learn this wisdom or, rather, as we laugh at its meagerness, we may slide by the mortal truth that Tristram has drawn us so close to.

While making the vast social adjustment, which these few examples may recall, Tristram has yet planted in his discourse, if not in the minds of his audience, the vital facts of his life and the essential humanity of his nature. As we have seen, Tristram preserves the peculiar Shandy flavor of his life while evolving from it a network of publicly relevant opinions; he asserts its tragedy while giving it a comic rendering; and he presents its basic sexual truths even while accommodating them to social prudery. Thus from Tristram's discourse, each reader may derive a vision of individual humanity's peculiarity, limitations, and dependence— if he will.

The essential, human truth of Tristram's life and its narrow social adjustment, then, live side by side throughout Sterne's novel. Since Sterne has never forced any interpretation from his readers —only wishing for wise ones (436)[1]—they may comfort one another with the wretched notion of Tristram as a nasty, trifling clown; or they may recognize, through Tristram's necessary social disguises, his profound humanity. The difference between these responses to Tristram's discourse is the measure of society's power over the minds of its individual members. But each member of society—each reader of Sterne's novel—shall decide for himself what the measure is.

CHAPTER 7

Transition

THE world in which Laurence Sterne wrote *A Sentimental Journey* was much larger than that one of a four-mile radius in which he commenced *Tristram Shandy*—and much sunnier.

Until 1750 Sterne had been successfully active in politics and society in the great northern city of York. But the years 1750 to 1759, in which *Tristram Shandy* was incubating, were a time of defeat and withdrawal for its author.[1] In 1751 Sterne's estranged uncle, Jacques Sterne, had exploited Laurence's troubles with his mother and put her "in that very place ['the common gaol'] where a hard report might do [him] . . . the most disservice."[2] In the wake of public disgrace, by which he was "bruised and humbled to the dust,"[3] Sterne retreated to his country parish at Sutton-in-the-Forest. The autobiographical digression in Volume I of *Tristram Shandy*, in which a grand confederacy of enemies smote the unsuspecting Yorick so that he fell as many a good man had fallen before and died broken-hearted, clearly shows Sterne's bitter view of society at this time: its powers—hypocritical, stupid, and grave—could join together and virtually murder defenseless merit. Sterne has gone too far here, of course: *he* did not die broken-hearted after all. But this undigested bitterness against society suggests the frame of mind in which Sterne conceived *Tristram Shandy* and explains, further, why he chose the novelistic form he did—that form which presents its hero constantly on the defensive against society.

Due to *Tristram Shandy's* success, however, the novelist was to be given a new lease on society. He followed his novel's first two volumes down to London in 1760 and enjoyed "an astonishing sequence of social triumphs."[4] Garrick promoted him; William Warburton, Bishop of Gloucester, gave him a purse of guineas; Hogarth gave him a frontispiece for his second edition; Reynolds painted his portrait; Pitt accepted his dedication; and old Lord Bathurst, who had given up all hope of again entertaining geniuses after the deaths of Pope and Swift, invited him to dinner. Sterne became so famous that a letter sent simply to "Tristram Shandy, Europe" reached him way up in Sutton. Indeed, the world of a four-mile radius in which he started *Tristram Shandy* had grown to include all of England and much of Europe before he concluded it. And it had become a generally smiling and flattering world.

Our recognizing this sunnier and more spacious social situation in which Sterne composed *A Sentimental Journey* should prepare us for its strikingly different presentation of Yorick and for its much happier view of man and society.

PART II

A Sentimental Journey

CHAPTER 8

Yorick's Sentimental Argument

THE eighteenth century, especially in its second half, was an empirical age, an age which attempted to base its general truths on what it took to be the only useful source of knowledge: experience and observation. It attempted to infer and to teach general truths by reference to as vast and representative a set of particular experiential cases as it could. David Hume, Sterne's great contemporary, celebrated the application to mankind of this empirical method in the introduction to his *Treatise of Human Nature:* ". . . As the science of man is the only solid foundation for the other sciences, so the only solid foundation we can give to this science itself must be laid on experience and observation." [1]

Samuel Johnson too, however much he disliked Hume's atheism, felt the same thing when he damned earlier fiction for its lack of "knowledge of nature, or acquaintance with life" and praised the fiction of his own day as arising "from general converse, and accurate observation of the living world." [2] His *Rasselas,* [3] for all its exotic trappings, develops from this relationship between general truths and observed items of evidence. [4] Johnson has begun it with the general opinion which it is his whole purpose to overthrow: "Ye who listen with credulity to the whispers of fancy, and persue with eagerness the phantoms of hope; who expect that age will perform the promises of youth, and that the deficiencies of the present day will be supplied by the morrow; attend to the history of Rasselas prince of Abissinia" (7).

Then Johnson follows with the particular experiences of this history, some reported, some sought out, and some stumbled across, which all add up to prove the vanity of such fancies and hopes. *Rasselas* works in this empirical way throughout. After attending to Imlac's particular experiences and his general inferences, Prince Rasselas says: ". . . whatever be the consequence of my experiment, I am resolved to judge, with my own eyes, of the various conditions of men, and then to make, deliberately, my *choice of life*" (48). His sister, the Princess Nekayah, also pursuing this method of study, makes her general statement that "Marriage has many pains, but celibacy has no pleasures" (83) only after a long, close observation of examples of both states. Rasselas and Nekayah are, of course, following in the footsteps of Imlac, whose general assertion that "Human life is everywhere a state, in which much is to be endured, and little to be enjoyed" (43) is based on a lifelong study of mankind almost from China to Peru.

The last sentences of the introduction to Hume's *Treatise* make really a better description of Johnson's fictional system in *Rasselas* than they do of the *Treatise:*

None of them [the natural sciences] can go beyond experience, or establish any principles which are not founded on that authority. Moral philosophy [that is, the science of human nature] has, indeed, this peculiar disadvantage, which is not found in natural, that in collecting its experiments, it cannot make them purposely, with premeditation, and after such a manner as to satisfy itself concerning every particular difficulty which may arise. When I am at a loss to know the effects of one body upon another in any situation, I need only put them in that situation, and observe what results from it. But should I endeavor to clear up after the same manner any doubt in moral philosophy, by placing myself in the same case with that which I consider, 'tis evident this reflection and premeditation would so disturb the operation of my natural principles, as must render it impossible to form any just conclusion from the phænomenon. We must therefore glean up our experiments in this science from a cautious observation of human life, and take them as they appear in the common course of the world, by men's behaviour in company, in affairs, and in their pleasures. Where experiments of this kind are judiciously collected and compared, we may hope to establish on them a science, which will not be inferior in certainty, and will be much superior in utility to any other of human comprehension.[5]

This makes an even more useful description of *A Sentimental Journey*[6] than it does of *Rasselas,* suggesting as it does the two major problems of our analysis: first, the nature of Parson Yorick's empirical system; and, second, the question of Parson Yorick's reliability as an observer and example.

Yorick's empirical system, we might note in passing, is an adaptation of the same vivid sensibility to the necessary interrelationship between particular experience and general truth which governed Sterne in his production of the life-opinions texture of *Tristram Shandy*.[7] The present adaptation is a set of sentimental experiences collected by Yorick from his recent French journey. The journey gave him the chance to try his affections on all the levels of society: on counts and ladies, gentle folk and business people, soldiers and priests, servants and peasants, charlatans and beggars. By stripping these experiments to their sentimental essentials and by composing each one so that its social meaning and value stand out most clearly, Yorick has presented us with a complete set of evidence on the social efficacy and worth of sentiment, hoping that the sum force of them all will be "to teach us to love the world and our fellow creatures better than we do." [8]

We cannot analyze the form of each item in Yorick's system; but it is important for us to have a sense of the "exquisite precision" [9] with which they have been individually organized and with which their social values have been defined.

I *Form and Technique*

One way by which Yorick has given each case its full meaning is to draw from various parts of his experience material which is relevant to the encounter immediately before him. He has filled in the story of his reconciliation with the old Franciscan monk, for instance, by adding to the story proper, first, something on the monk's early misfortunes and, then, his own later mourning over the monk's grave (44-45). This completes the story of his relationship with the monk, making a little vignette which shows the justness and the durability of Yorick's final regard for the monk. Yorick has similarly filled in his account of the starling by putting down, just after the story of their encounter, the bird's past and its future history (110-11). Sometimes Yorick has worked into his individual French adventures material of merely thematic relevance, as when he adds to the story of the poor Chevalier that of the noble Breton—"because the two stories reflect light upon each other" (116-18). Yorick has added to his discovery of La

Fleur's susceptibility to love and to his consequent description of
love's effect on himself the fragment on love's power over the Ab-
derites (62-63), thus composing a little essay on the power of
love.

Yorick has organized other sections of his book, not in terms of
likes, but of unlikes. This arrangement sometimes amounts only
to his emphasizing contrasts that his travels themselves have produced, such as his shyness and the little debonaire French captain's confident gallantry toward the Flemish lady (48-49), the
galloping and then the plodding of the post horses between Nampont and Amiens (71-72), and his sharp shift of feeling, on the
Franciscan's first appearance, from generosity to stinginess (24-
26). He heightens the contrast between himself and the little captain by closing it with the vivid sense he had of it at the time it
happened; and that between the horses' galloping and plodding by
representing himself as having predicted the shift just before it
came. Other contrasts, such as that between his own sentimental
outwardness and the sour introversion of Smelfungus and Mundungus (54-56), Yorick has had to compose, bringing together
experiences and feelings from different periods of his travels.

Still a third way by which Yorick defines the separate elements
of his sentimental experience, besides composing sections of similar and of contrasting material, is that of generalization. He has
concluded his account of the courteous grisset's husband by a general piece of advice to all such men to enter more into society
(86), his description of La Fleur's holiday plans by pointing out
the spiritual easiness of all servants (139), and his meeting with
Maria by a general exaltation of the sensibility which his sympathy for her exemplifies (160-61). He has introduced his encounter with the courteous grisset with an invocation to courtesy
(82), and the incident of the dwarf at the Opera Comique with
a general discourse on dwarfs (92-93).

Yorick has composed several sections of his travels by using
both comparison and generalization. In his essay on the translation of gestures, for instance, Yorick generalizes his correct interpretation of the old French officer's response to his first entering
the theater box and then follows with a similar experience, his
correct interpretation of the Marquisina di F***'s backward
glance toward himself at a concert in Milan—this latter further

exemplifying Yorick's generalization (89-91). The chapter entitled *"The Rose"* is similar in form, having been composed of a present experience, the *grossierté* of the poor Abbé in one of the upper loges, a general statement based on it, that we should tolerate the *grossiertés* of other people and nations, and then another exemplary experience, Yorick's recollection of the gross way the chaste Madame Rambouliet asked to pluck a rose (96-97). The only formal difference between this chapter and that on gestural translation is that the centrally located general statement is here doubled, being spoken first as a plea by the old French officer and then echoed as an avowal by the sentimental traveler. A more extensive version of this formal pattern is the section on flattery. There a particular revelation of flattery's wonderful effect, a revelation which is held off through three disjointed chapters (133-34;137;149-51), leads Yorick to a general statement on the power of flattery (152) and finally to a number of particular applications (153-55).

These highly individual items of sentimental experience are usually defined by chapter breaks and chapter headings. However, single chapters will often cast reflections on one another, thus forming longer units—as in the case of the three chapters on the dead ass (67-72). The first chapter, *"The Bidet,"* presents, first, La Fleur's ascendingly severe curses at the dead ass, and, second, a general discourse of Yorick's on French cursing. The second chapter, *"Nampont—The Dead Ass,"* describes the peasant who owned and mourns the ass, tells the peasant's story of his friendship with the ass, and, after giving a brief exchange between Yorick and the peasant, ends with Yorick's general pronouncement: "Shame on the world! said I to myself—Did we love each other, as this poor soul but loved his ass—'twould be something.—" The third chapter, *"Nampont—The Postillion,"* is composed of the galloping-plodding contrast already discussed, with Yorick fretting while the horses gallop and sleeping while they plod; and it closes with a brief transition, Yorick's waking up and rubbing his eyes at Amiens.

We have here, then, three sharply defined items, a time gap separating the first two and a sharp change in condition and in characters separating the second from the third; and they are three individually formed items too, each one organized of well-knit, interrelated parts. And yet they are also related variously to one another: we have one contrast between the dead ass as an indifferent or annoying object and then as an object of love; a second between Yorick's feelings for the dead ass and his indifference to the hard-whipped horses; and a third between the great depth of Yorick's feelings and their very short duration. All of these are presented more sharply because of the sharp definitions of the total adventure's separate parts.

The separate items of Yorick's experience are also connected by a very slight narrative thread. Yorick set out for the Opera Comique, for instance, because his barber had made him too late to visit Madame R****; he stopped to ask the way of the courteous grisset; he went to the bookstore on the way back because something he had heard there made him want to buy a copy of Shakespeare's works (80-101). This slight narrative connection does not disturb each item's integrity: each one has its own special cast of characters, its own form, and its own social significance. Their patterns are softened a little, however, by other discursive material than the particular social narrations and the generalizations which are their basic substances: that is, by such things as fragmentary anecdotes and dialogues. But these are usually highly polished too. There is, for instance, the anecdote of the notary who went from a domestic storm to an actual storm (144-47), Yorick's talk on love to Madame de L*** (51-52), and his conversation on the French with the Count de B**** (127-128). Neither their narrative connections, then, nor their mixture with more fluid literary materials smudges the patterns of Yorick's individual items of sentimental experience.

Yorick has carefully cut away from between each of them, furthermore, all purely private and travel information which would have diluted their sentimental content and smudged their outlines. He has filled the gaps of unrecorded time between sentimental encounters with only enough transition to keep his readers informed, using such short-hand connectives as "in half an hour we got to the post-house at Nampont" (68) and "When I got to my hotel" (102). Sometimes when the joint between two items is or will soon become plain, Yorick has given us no transition at all (89;156). Yorick has once or twice acknowledged events in these nonsentimental gaps: his having trouble with his luggage between Calais and Montriul (57) and the odd train of thoughts which led him from the Opera Comique to the bookstore (98). He has jokingly filled in a couple of others: one with an extraneous story (117-18) and one with sleep (72). But in these cases, as throughout the book, Yorick has helped us see the essential separateness of the different events—their difference in characters and in situation and their being unpredictable one from another— with chapter breaks and chapter headings.

A Sentimental Journey, then, is a microcosm of separate social experiences, each one radiant with its own social meaning and all adding up, by empirical inference, to the great lesson of "NATURE, and those affections which arise out of her, which make us love each other—and the world, better than we do" (121).

II *Sentimentality*

Before rehearsing Yorick's empirical argument for the universal practice of these sentimental affections, however, it might be wise to define sentimentality. Sentimentality, as Yorick understands it, is a broad general affection—a principle of benevolence which emanates miscellaneously from each human breast outward to encompass all others. It seems to be the essential cement for all human society, being capable by particular modifications of realizing itself as pity, love, fellow-feeling, loyalty, generosity, tolerance, and so forth. Yorick's creator has often invoked such a general human affection in his sermons, although he has not called it sentimentality. Jesus, Sterne has said, put "the love of our neighbor upon its true bottom of philanthropy and universal kindness." [10] Again he says: "Could Christianity persuade the professors of it . . . to go on and exalt our natures, and . . . to plant [in the place of unfriendliness] all those . . . humane and benevolent inclinations, which . . . should dispose us to extend our love and goodness to our fellow creatures," then this world would be a preview of paradise. [11] This statement chimes perfectly, by the way, with the one that Yorick makes on the old German's love of his ass (70). Sterne, in still another sermon, found that it was native human benevolence which held fast the bands of society. [12] The notion which stands out in all these references was nicely reflected by Walter Sichel when he wrote that Sterne's feeling was rather *toward* human beings than *for* them, that his "taper sent out its glow to all humanity and persons were only details." [13]

Yorick's definition of a sentimental traveler as one who neither fears nor disdains to walk alone down a dark passageway (149), which overlies the feeling of a general trust and concern for all human beings, perfectly agrees with Sterne's advocacy of a general benevolence. So does Yorick's notion that a man must have "a sort of an affection" for all women to love any one woman as he ought (120).[14] Sterne and Yorick also agree that the love for one woman extends itself into a general affection for all humanity. "I must ever have some Dulcinea in my head," Sterne has written in a letter: "it harmonizes the soul." [15] And Yorick, typically, sharpens this statement when he rejoices to hear that La Fleur is an incurable lover of women:

I am heartily glad of it, said I—'twill save me the trouble every night of putting my breeches under my head. In saying this, I was making not so much La Fleur's eloge, as my own, having been in love, with one princess or other, almost all my life, and I hope I shall go on so till I die, being firmly persuaded, that if ever I do a mean action, it must be in some interval betwixt one passion and another: whilst this interregnum lasts, I always perceive my heart locked up—I can scarce find in it to give Misery a sixpence; and therefore I always get out of it as fast as I can, and the moment I am rekindled, I am all generosity and goodwill again. . . . (62)

Sentiment then is a general feeling of affection which underlies all one's particular affections and is reinforced by them.

III *Method of Instruction*

Sterne's method of teaching sentiment in *A Sentimental Journey* is exemplary, empirical. His teacher, Parson Yorick, can proclaim the general social efficacy of sentiment because in every variety of social encounter his sentimental practices have allowed him to give and to receive the blessings of society. These blessings are not material, of course, for Yorick's sentimental outlays—eight sous to the beggars at Montriul, the purchase of one paté (which was worth the price) from the Chevalier, a crown (which she is not going to spend) to the fair *fille de chambre,* the offer of a place in his coach to Madame de L*** (an offer she could not accept)—do not amount to very much. The sentimental blessings are social and personal. They are such things as Yorick's charming flirtations with women of all classes, his sharing of tears with Maria, the noble Breton, and with the German peasant; his pleasant conversations with the old French officer, the Count de B****, and the peasant patriarch; his connection with the Marquisina di F***; his reconciliation with the old Franciscan; and La Fleur's loyalty. Whenever Yorick has given free play to his sentimental affections—in high places and low, in country and city, among men and women—he has given and received such pleasures as these. In those few cases where bigotry or prudence or social ambition blocked his affections, Yorick has made himself and usually those around him unhappy.

To realize the full radiance of Yorick's social pleasures we might compare his public charity at Montriul with James Boswell's much more ambitious public charity in London.

SATURDAY 8 JANUARY. I forgot to mention that upon Thursday I went to Michael Cholmondeley and gave him four shillings, three from the Kellie family and one of my own. The creature did not seem so thankful as I could wish. An old woman who stood by (for I gave him it in a little court) grumbled that I might have bestowed my charity better, and presently a young one said that people who had both been worthless and would be idle should not be encouraged. Michael's choler rose, he raged in blackguard exclamation. The young jade said he had fifty wives or thereabouts, and such as encouraged him would choose to have the like. By this time a number of miscreants was gathered round us. I was sorely beset, and stood like the unhappy stag at bay, considering how it should come about that I should be thus rendered uneasy when in the exercise of that most Christian grace, charity. A Scotch Seceder or an English Methodist would make out many mystical conjectures on this subject. They would affirm that it was a temptation of Satan in order to try my steadfastness, and if possible drive me from the practice of goodness. Or perhaps that Providence had permitted the infernal enemy of souls to assault me, on purpose to teach me that I should be more judicious and less whimsical in the exercise of my benevolence. I endeavored to expostulate with the two incensed females in terms mild and gentle. "You see," said I, "this poor old man. We shall not dispute whether his conduct has been good. But you see him ragged, hungry, and cold; and surely I did right in trying to relieve a fellow-creature in such circumstances." I then stole away slowly from them. Their malevolence and hardness of heart I detested, yet I imagine the creature Cholmondeley must have been worthless. I asked a decent tradesman before whose shop we stood what character he had. "Sir," said he, with a kind of waggery, "he is a very honest man from head to foot." [16]

This, Yorick might say, is the difference in social pleasure between one who has achieved the sentimental style and one who has not. And what has worked for me, he would go on to say, will work for you.

CHAPTER 9

Yorick's Reliability

B UT it is questionable, one will say, whether Sterne would have us follow Yorick's lesson. Surely Sterne often shows Yorick's sentimental practices to be absurd, doubly absurd when, as often happens, Yorick does not even see how foolish he has been. And surely we should think twice before following a foolish model or attending an uncritical teacher. To face this important question we must study the absurdities in Yorick's sentimentality and then see if Sterne's handling of Yorick and of Yorick's situation alleviates them.

I *Yorick's Sentimental Absurdity*

Yorick's sentimental affections are absurd for three main reasons: their generality; their unsteady ebbs and flows; and their mixture with self-love. Let us consider these three forms of sentimental absurdity separately.

Yorick's feelings are, no doubt, absurdly broad, covering not only the whole of humanity, but melancholy trees (54), a caged starling (106), and a deserted old desobligeant (36). His willingness to maintain his general feelings when he might easily refine them is especially ridiculous. We cite his happy relaxation in his vague feelings about the lady he met in Calais, for instance: "Having, on the first sight of the lady, settled the affair in my fancy, 'that she was of the better order of beings'—and then laid it down as a second axiom, as indisputable as the first, that she was a widow, and wore a character of distress—I went no further; I got ground enough for the situation which pleased me—and had she remained close beside my elbow till midnight, I should have held true to my system, and considered her only under that general idea" (48). Yorick was absurdly ready to act on such feelings: hiring La Fleur, for instance, because of his weakness for any poor devil who offers "his service to so poor a devil as myself"—only to discover that La Fleur's only talents are for drum beating and spatterdash making (59-60).

Yorick does, however, have some sense of the need to sharpen his sentiments, even those towards the lady he met in Calais. In attacking Frenchmen's use of sentiments—that is, their use of general all-purpose professions of passion and fidelity—or rather, in showing the lady how general sentiments must be modified to fit each woman, Yorick softens our impression of him as a mere taper of sentiment. He shows the same sense of a need to refine his sentiments when he argues with himself over how to address the Duc de C**** (112-13). We also see Yorick actually make particular adjustments: in his softening response to the girl with the box of lace (135-36), in his achievement of kinder feelings toward Monsieur Dessein (38); and in his submission to the peasant family's odd style of saying grace (164). However, he always begins an adventure in his vastly imprecise sentimental way, approaching the old French captain, for instance, with fond memories of Captain Tobias Shandy (89), visiting the Count de B**** because the count likes all Englishmen (114), and searching out Maria "in quest of melancholy adventures" (156). And he commonly proceeds in his friendships on little other than such general, imprecise feelings as these reveal: on a friendliness for all anglophiles and old soldiers, a sympathy for all examples of misery in distress, a kindness for all pretty women. He seldom knows much about his acquaintance; he seldom seeks for more knowledge than enough to free his affections; and he never lets his lack of knowledge keep him from deep soul-satisfying feelings and professions.

Yorick's sentimental practice is also absurd in its sudden ebbs and flows. His first adventure, that with the old Franciscan (24-26), was ruined when the high tide of generosity he had been professing completely ebbed away on the monk's appearance. Equally striking is the displacement of Yorick's sympathy for the dead ass and its owner by his annoyance at the hasty postillion, especially since he was annoyed not at the whipping the postillion was giving his horses, but merely at being shaken out of his soulful feelings about the ass (69-72). Yorick's feelings for women were almost mechanical, running high when one was present and ebbing the moment she departed. He said easily, just after the interesting Madame de L*** was drawn out of his way, "What a large volume of adventures may be grasped within this little span of life, by him who interests his heart in every thing, and who, having eyes to see what time and chance are perpetually holding out to him as he journeyeth on his way, misses nothing he can *fairly* lay his hands on.—[¶]—If this won't turn out something—another will—no matter—'tis an assay upon human nature —I get my labour for my pains—'tis enough—the pleasure of the experiment has kept my senses and the best part of my blood awake, and laid the gross to sleep" (54). His feeling for the lovely and pitiful Maria lasted a little longer: "There was nothing from which I had painted out for myself so joyous a riot of the affections, as in this journey in the vintage, through this part of France; but pressing through this gate of sorrow to it, my sufferings have totally unfitted me: in every scene of festivity I saw Maria in the background of the piece, sitting pensive under her poplar; and I had got almost to Lyons before I was able to cast a shade across her" (161). Almost to Lyons! Even his eternal love for Eliza was subject to Yorick's sentimental giddiness: it ebbed when he came across some other pretty woman and flowed when Yorick was again alone (73-74;160).

More absurd and more damaging to Yorick's value as a sentimental exemplar is the ever-present mixture of self-love with his sentimental affections. No matter how high the tide of sentiment flows, some tincture of selfishness stains and adulterates it. Yorick's sympathy for the dead ass, the Chevalier, the beggars, and the noble Breton was always, at least in part, a self-indulgence in fine feelings. His feeling for the fair *fille de chambre*, for all its paternal trimmings, and that for the grisset, for all its courtesies, were compromised by lust. His reconciliation with the monk was partially a display of Yorick's goodness for the Flemish lady's benefit; and his courtly friendship with the Count de B**** had a request for a favor tied to it. Yorick has explicitly faced his mixture of feelings once in his travels, during the conquest of his lust for the fair *fille de chambre* (132); but this one moment of self-awareness has not prevented the sentimental traveler from his most shameless display of self-seeking, his brilliantly successful practice of flattery (153-55), nor—when that ended in self-disgust—from an uncritical indulgence in his mixed feelings of sympathy, soul-tickling, and lust toward Maria.

Through Yorick's inability to escape these absurd elements in his sentimental practice, even after he has acknowledged them, Sterne seems to be saying that sentimentality is inescapably absurd. This interpretation is what some of Sterne's most perceptive critics have also apparently felt. A *Sentimental Journey*, says Rufus Putney, is "a hoax by which Sterne persuaded his contemporaries that the humor he wanted to write was the pathos they wished to read." [1] And Ernest Dilworth concurs, stating that this book is really "highly inventive mockery of pity and fellow-feeling." [2] Thus we are asked to take Yorick's set of sentimental instances not as an empirical proof of sentiment's general social value, but as a proof of its general absurdity. There is truth in this, but it would be strange if Sterne, who "would have withered and blown away . . . without society and its artifices," as Mr. Dilworth says,[3] had meant for us to leave the matter here.

II   *The Sense to Yorick's Sentiment*

If we look again at Sterne's handling of Yorick and of Yorick's situation, we will see how to admit Yorick's absurdity and yet accept him as a teacher and an example.

First of all, Sterne has presented his sentimental hero, for all his follies, as an extremely attractive, charming figure. Yorick made an elegant appearance, for instance, in his French-English conversations with the Count de B****, and a very sly and graceful one in his flirtation with Madame de L***; he was wonderfully amiable in his talk with the old French officer and in his visit with the peasant family below Mount Taurira. He has likewise endured his little disgraces, such as the expedient by which he wrote Madame de L*** when his wit had failed him and the unlucky figure he made in his passport, with wonderful humor and grace. There is a brilliance, an aura, about Yorick even when he is exhibited in such questionable activities as his parcelling out eight sous to sixteen beggars, trading snuff boxes with the monk, and engaging in the beggarly practice of flattery.

Yorick's charm is not, however, merely a show; for it is firmly based on his candor and honesty. Yorick is willing to tell such things as his fiasco with the Franciscan (25-29), his excessive charity to the *pauvre honteux* (65), his public counting of the grisset's pulse (84), and the peculiar identification on his passport (125-26) even though these things, as he explicitly acknowledges, may show him in a bad light. Of course, Yorick's easy candor often heightens the laughter against him, as Mr. Putney and Mr. Dilworth have pointed out. We laugh at Yorick's story of glove buying, for instance, because he has revealed toward the grisset a strong sexual pull of which he seems hardly aware. With his revelation of the Flemish lady's influence on his feelings and actions toward the old monk at Calais (30), Yorick has put himself in the same absurd light. He has done so, yet again, by completing the history of the starling, which, as Mr. Putney has noticed,[4] belies his promise to free it (110-11).

But Yorick's candor is not always a means merely of exposing himself to laughter; often it is an element of clear-sighted intelligence. Yorick knew how foolish he would seem in hiring La Fleur so rashly as he did (59), in giving so much to the *pauvre honteux,* and in cribbing his letter to Madame de L*** (75-78). He has preceded his account of his meeting with Maria, again, by admitting its quixotic absurdity (156); and he immediately followed the elaborate vow of fidelity he had made to Eliza by asserting severely, "In transports of this kind, the heart, in spite of the understanding, will always say too much" (74). We may laugh at Yorick, the sentimental traveler; but we often do so at the direction of Yorick, the critical memorialist.

Sterne has also given Yorick, the sentimental traveler, more wit and greater powers of self-knowledge than we may be inclined to recognize. His mental struggles are often presented allegorically, as in his considering whether or not to invite the Flemish lady to share his coach (46-47). Every "bad propensity" in his nature—Avarice, Caution, Cowardice, Discretion, Hypocrisy, Meanness and Pride—argued against this act of friendliness and generosity; but Yorick's better nature won out. The fact that Yorick's good in this struggle is probably the reader's bad only heightens the sense it gives of Yorick's vivid awareness of the social problem confronting him. Another allegorical representation of the traveler's lively consciousness is that over his address to the Duc de C****:

Then nothing would serve me, when I got within sight of Versailles, but putting words and sentences together, and conceiving attitudes and tones to wreath myself into Monsieur le Duc de C****'s good graces—This will do, said I—Just as well, retorted I again, as a coat carried up to him by an adventurous taylor, without taking his measure—Fool! continued I,—see Monsieur le Duc's face first—observe what character is written in it—take notice in what posture he stands to hear you—mark the turns and expressions of his body and limbs—and for the tone—the first sound which comes from his lips will give it you; and from all these together you'll compound an address at once upon the spot, which cannot disgust the Duke—the ingredients are his own, and most likely to go down.

Well! said I, I wish it well over—Coward again! as if man to man was not equal throughout the whole surface of the globe; and if in the field—why not face to face in the cabinet too? And trust me, Yorick, whenever it is not so, man is false to himself, and betrays his own succours ten times where nature does it once. Go to the Duc de C**** with the Bastile in thy looks—My life for it, thou wilt be sent back to Paris in half an hour with an escort.

I believe so, said I—Then I'll go to the Duke, by Heaven! with all the gaiety and debonairness in the world.—

—And there you are wrong again, replied I—a heart at ease, Yorick, flies into no extremes—'tis ever on its centre—Well! well! cried I, as the coachman turn'd in at the gates, I find I shall do very well.   (112-13)

There are several other such descriptions of the traveler's active mind: his argument with his own wisdom in the hiring of La Fleur (59-60); his victory over the avarice and mistrust that arise in him against Monsieur Dessein (38); and his final control of his base desire for revenge on the Parisian *maître d' hôtel* (135-36).

Sterne has labored, then, to give his hero the dignity that comes with public grace, honesty, and intelligence—a dignity that may befit him as a model and a teacher. His many displays of good sense as a traveler and the corrections of his follies which he makes as a memorialist should leave him with us as a man who bears himself and understands himself better than most of us.

We can test Sterne's success in endowing Yorick with personal dignity by referring to his near seduction of the fair *fille de chambre*. After "*The Temptation—Paris,*" during which Yorick has described the stages by which his passions were aroused and the innocent girl upset on his bed, there comes:

The Conquest

Yes—and then—Ye whose clay-cold heads and lukewarm hearts can argue down or mask your passions, tell me, what trespass is it that man should have them? or how his spirit stands answerable to the Father of spirits but for his conduct under them.

If Nature has so wove her web of kindness that some threads of love and desire are entangled with the piece—must the whole web be rent in drawing them out?—Whip me such stoics, great Governor of nature! said I to myself—Wherever thy providence shall place me for the trials of my virtue—whatever is my danger—whatever is my situation—let me feel the movements which rise out of it, and which belong to me as a man—and if I govern them as a good one, I will trust the issues to thy justice: for thou hast made us, and not we ourselves.

As I finish'd my address, I raised the fair *fille de chambre* up by the hand, and led her out of the room—she stood by me till I lock'd the door and put the key in my pocket—*and then*—the victory being quite decisive—and not till then, I press'd my lips to her cheek, and taking her by the hand again, led her safe to the gate of the hotel. (132)

I agree with Herbert Read in accepting Yorick's reversal, in feeling him to possess the dignity which allows him to take such high ground after so near a fall.[5] Surely Sterne, who so richly labored both the traveler's and the writer's intelligent honesty and who has presented this speech as both the traveler's to himself and as the writer's to his audience, has the right to expect us to take Yorick at his word.

But, one may respond, Yorick is still a comic figure. Even if he has here faced the selfish mixture in his social feelings for once, he never cures it any more than he cures those feelings' gross generality: his easy mingling of tears with Maria, his passport, his cribbing of the corporal's lecherous letter, and his chaste attendance on Madame de Rambouliet are all inescapably, inexcusably funny. This is true; but I believe Sterne has given us strong reasons for approving and practicing such mixed and such general social sentiments as Yorick's practice exemplifies, absurd though they sometimes are.

Yorick himself has explained in *"The Conquest"* why we must socialize from motives mixed with selfishness: it is because ". . . Nature has so wove her web of kindness that some threads of love and desire are entangled with the piece." Nature has given us impure social emotions; emotions which are susceptible of selfish ebbs and flows, and, even at their height, indissolubly mixed with self-love. ". . . There is nothing unmix'd in this world" (126). Yorick's assertion of such a mixture as essential to human nature fits the teaching of the whole eighteenth century that all human beings and all human institutions are mixed and impure. One may remember Martin's coat, Swift's allegorical representation of the Anglican Church, for example: its fabric was so embroidered, so interwoven with ribbons, knots, laces, linings, and figures that Martin could not draw them all out without destroying his coat in the operation.[6] Or, to come closer to Yorick, we find Pope in his *Essay on Man* telling us:

> Two Principles in human nature reign;
> Self-love, to urge, and Reason, to restrain;
> Nor this a good, nor that a bad we call,
> Each works its end, to move or govern all:
> And to their proper operation still,
> Ascribe all Good; to their improper, Ill.
> Self-love, the spring of motion, acts the soul;
> Reason's comparing balance rules the whole.
> Man, but for that, no action could attend,
> And but for this, were active to no end:
> Fixed like a plant on his peculiar spot,
> To draw nutrition, propagate, and rot;
> Or, meteor-like, flame lawless through the void,
> Destroying others, by himself destroyed.[7]

Sterne is not speaking so broadly in *A Sentimental Journey* as Pope, nor so cheerily; but he is insisting on the same ancient wisdom. Any sympathy or friendship for a man must include service of some kind or allow some kind of spiritual tickling; any kindness for a woman is partly a matter of sexual lust. Through case upon case of Yorick's mixed social feelings, Sterne teaches us what his hero consciously admits in *"The Conquest"*: that one must follow mixed motives in his social addresses or avoid society.

But why must a man practice such absurdly general senti-ments? The fragmentary nature of Yorick's adventures, suggestive of the fragmentary nature of all social experience, explains that. None of the brief, sharply isolated adventures which Yorick re-veals chance and travel to have given and taken away from him allowed him to try for a perfect knowledge of any of his ac-quaintance. He saw very few of them more than once; virtually all his planned second meetings fell through; and all his acquaint-ance were quickly drawn away from him. But it was not simply the chancy business of travel that made Yorick's acquaintance with others so slight and fragmentary. Yorick shared very few ex-periences and feelings even with his faithful La Fleur, as the epi-sode of the old French fragment shows. La Fleur rushed out, at Yorick's command, to fetch the paper on which was written the rest of the notary's story, La Fleur having used the paper, whose writing so excited Yorick, to wrap a nosegay for his new mistress:

> In a very little time the poor fellow came back quite out of breath, with deeper marks of disappointment in his looks than could arise from the simple irreparability of the fragment—*Juste ciel!* in less than two minutes that the poor fellow had taken his last tender farewell of her—his faithless mistress had given his *gage d' amour* to one of the Count's footman—the footman to a young sempstress—and the sempstress to a fiddler, with my fragment at the end of it—Our misfortunes were in-volved together—I gave a sigh—and La Fleur echo'd it back again to my ear.
> —How perfidious! cried La Fleur—How unlucky! said I.
> —I should not have been mortified, Monsieur, quoth La Fleur, if she had lost it—Nor I, La Fleur, said I, had I found it.   (148)

Despite their apparently close and continuous companionship, Yorick and La Fleur are utterly divided; they can share almost none of one another's hopes and griefs.

The brief fragmentary social experiences of Yorick's journey should remind us that we are not omniscient gods who grasp per-fectly the total natures and feelings of those around us, but lim-ited beings who depend on our brief and flickering experience for what little we know. How limited our experience and knowl-edge are, any of Sterne's contemporaries can teach us. We may think of Hume's brilliant chapter "Of scepticism with regard to the senses," [8] for instance, or of Johnson's remark that "no man can, at the same time, fill his cup from the source and from the mouth of the Nile." [9] Yorick's journey further teaches that we are not trees who enjoy an unbroken communion with a few fellows north, south, east, and west, but rootless wanderers whose meetings with one another, even in our most settled states, are brief, chancy and disjointed. We always start a friendship in ignorance and we always proceed sketchily informed. If we wish to start, then, what must we do? Sterne teaches us that we must love mankind better than we do; that is, we must begin a friendship with generally friendly feelings to begin at all. Of course, we should respond to particular experiences and refine our feelings and addresses as knowledge grows. Yorick has advocated this in his prescription for love-making and in his monologue on addressing the Duc de C****. In his conduct, especially in his conversation with the old French captain, and in his visit with the peasant family, he has given us good examples. But human knowledge can never be complete.

This then is Sterne's extremely unsentimental social teaching. If we want to enjoy those social sweets for which nature has given us such an appetite, we must accept nature's conditions. Since she allows us so brief and incomplete a knowledge of others, we must always begin a friendship and often continue it on the ground of a general feeling of benevolence: we must be sympathetic to griefs we cannot share and tolerant of customs we cannot understand. Since she has given us no pure social sentiments, we must proceed from sentiments which are clouded and tinctured with selfishness. Of course, in following such mixed and such general social sentiments we continually court absurdity and embarrassment; but our natural need for society and the chances of such social pleasures as Yorick has enjoyed show that the risk is worthwhile. And what is the alternative for those who hope to avoid being laughed at?—Smelfungus and Mundungus.

With the laughable but charming Yorick Sterne teaches that it is better to risk embarrassment, better even to be absurdly foolish sometimes, than to ride alone in a desobligeant, scowling forever through a scowling and desolate world.

CHAPTER 10

Conclusion

MANY English novelists have evolved their narratives from favorite concerns, favorite points of creative departure, and evocative reference. Jane Austen started, characteristically, with problems of courtship and marriage; Tobias Smollett with the alien's confrontation of the socio-economic establishment; George Eliot with the gifted soul's, especially the gifted woman's, problems of social adjustment and social contribution. Each of these three novelists has given his work its power and coherence and achieved his vision of society by following out his own vividly realized point of interest. Thus, every word and action of Elizabeth Bennet relates to the question of her marriageableness; every adventure of Roderick Random is a win or a loss against the establishment; every choice of Dorothea will be seen to advance or depress her social adjustment and utility.

Laurence Sterne also started from a favorite concern, a favorite narrative seed. His concern, a supremely natural one in eighteenth-century England, is the confrontation of polite society by the individual social consciousness. Sterne has evolved *Tristram Shandy* from one aspect of this concern: from the limitations polite society imposes on personal expression. This novel develops through its whole length the conversational stress a gentleman endures when he is torn between the need to ingratiate himself with society and the need to share with its members the truth in his heart. Sterne has given this stress an absolute emphasis by presenting his conversational hero, on the one hand, with an extremely sensitive social consciousness and, on the other, with a vital communication whose facts are almost all socially unsuitable. He has made this sharply articulated point of stress, moreover, the unavoidable center of his novel. His reader, who lacks the assistance of the omniscient commentary that eases most "conversational" novels and the protection of foolish commentary—except for the brief and guarded queries of Madam and Sir—cannot avoid even for a minute extensive involvement in Tristram's discursive problems and solutions. He finds himself implicated in all of Tristram's dodges, reversals, equivocations, and innuendoes. There is no one to explain away the thoughts that Tristram raises in his mind and no one but himself to take the blame for them.

It is in large part this sense of involvement, I believe, that underlies the frequent suggestions critics have made that *Tristram Shandy* has a tragic coloration. Even if the reader considers Tristram's situation and utterance purely comical, he finds that the implications and the focus of its laughter endanger and frighten him. Any laugh he allows himself may muddy his sense of his own social respectability; any laugh he denies himself erodes his sense of his own personal honesty. Since, then, the reader finds himself sharing Tristram's social perils, he cannot take these perils lightly. And his awareness of the unmentionable facts underlying these perils may add pity to fear, and cement the impression that he is, however strange it may seem, tragically involved in a comic situation.

A Sentimental Journey focusses on a different aspect of the gentleman-society confrontation from *Tristram Shandy*. It takes up not the problems and limitations of polite expression but the difficulties and the chances of polite communion. *Tristram Shandy* concerns substantial communication between the members of society; *A Sentimental Journey* concerns only social conviviality. In *A Sentimental Journey* Sterne has presented the prejudice, the suspicion, and the ignorance that keep one person from enjoying the company of others; and he has suggested the practice of a universal feeling of benevolence as a possible solution. Sterne's address to his audience in *A Sentimental Journey* also differs from that in *Tristram Shandy*. By setting the basic material of this novel—Yorick's sentimental adventures—in the lucid stream of Yorick's travel memoir, Sterne gives us the detachment, the emotional distance, necessary for us to judge Yorick's laughable teaching and example. The critical eye Yorick casts over his sentimental activity and the perfect clarity of his narration allow us, whether we approve or only laugh, to remain perfectly uninvolved with Yorick. Only for a moment, in *"The*

Conquest," does he make the kind of a claim on his reading public that the conversational Tristram continuously makes. The effect of that moment, about which each reader shall decide for himself, is very important and, for my part, decisive in Yorick's favor. But for the rest, the reader's withers are unwrung. Tristram involves us in the problems of polite conversation; Yorick sets us off at the distance of laughter to consider the problems of polite communion.

It is, of course, this social dynamics, which is the essence of his art, that Sterne's many imitators, like most of his critics, have neglected or misunderstood. His followers of the late eighteenth and early nineteenth centuries, such as Henry Mackenzie, commonly slipped into the muddle of sentiment; those of more recent times, such as George Meredith and James Joyce, have gone off the deep end of whimsy and private association. Of course, such a misunderstanding, when it is a literary genius like Joyce who misunderstands, can lead to remarkable results, to new creations which have their own inner dynamics. But *Ulysses* descends no more legitimately from *Tristram Shandy* than *The Man of Feeling* does from *A Sentimental Journey.* All the materials of Sterne's art—the odd opinions, the whimsical humor, the bawdy suggestiveness, the sentimental benevolence—when they are not subjected to the rigors of social necessity, dwindle into prettiness, sweetness, and worse. Even Sterne's brilliantly conversational style, which flows strongly through nineteenth-century narrative prose, when it is not used to project conversational stress and social awareness, becomes merely a neat, pretty way of writing. It is historically true that these abuses of Sterne's materials and Sterne's techniques have helped cast shadows over Sterne's great achievements; but they need not and should not do so. Neither Joyce's wonderful composition of private human consciousness nor Mackenzie's tear-jerkers should blind us to the public, social encounters of *Tristram Shandy* and *A Sentimental Journey.*

It would be extravagant to say that Laurence Sterne's two great novels have exhausted the literary potential of so lively and enduring a human concern as this one of polite confrontation. But two-hundred years after their composition, *Tristram Shandy* and *A Sentimental Journey* still focus this concern with unrivalled depth, precision, and emotional power.

[115]

Notes and References

Preface

1. All the books mentioned in the Preface are listed in my Bibliography.

2. Sterne's own words in the brief memoir he wrote for his daughter; see Wilbur Cross, *The Life and Times of Laurence Sterne* (New Haven, 1929), p. 15 for these words, and pp. 12-15 for extensive quotation of the memoir.

Chapter One

1. See Wayne C. Booth, "The Self-conscious Narrator in Prose Fiction before *Tristram Shandy*," *PMLA*, LXVII (1952), 163-85; and Booth's unpubl. disc., "*Tristram Shandy* and its Precursors," (Chicago, 1950) for the history of the self-conscious narrator.

2. *On English Prose* (Toronto, 1957), p. 79.

3. *The Life and Times of Laurence Sterne* (New Haven, 1929), p. 542.

4. *The Second Common Reader* (New York, 1932), p. 81.

5. *Diderot and Sterne* (New York, 1955), pp. 193; 194-95.

6. See A. S. Pringle-Pattison's "Introduction" to his edition of John Locke, *An Essay Concerning Human Understanding* (Oxford, 1950), p. xxviii on Locke's essentially minor interest in the principle of association. To simplify the reader's study of this matter or, rather, to attempt to put this old hobbyhorse of *Tristram Shandy* criticism out of its misery, I submit the following material: first, an extensive quotation on association from Locke's *Essay*, I. ed. A. C. Fraser (Oxford, 1849), 527-33, and, second, a discussion of association in *Tristram Shandy*.

FROM "OF THE ASSOCIATION OF IDEAS"

(1) There is scarce any one that does not observe something that seems odd to him, and is in itself really extravagant, in the opinions, reasonings, and

Something unreasonable in most Men.

actions of other men. The least flaw of this kind, if at all different from his own, every one is quick-sighted enough to espy in another, and will by the authority of reason forwardly condemn; though he be guilty of much greater unreasonableness in his own tenets and conduct, which he never perceives, and will very hardly, if at all, be convinced of.

(2) This proceeds not wholly from self-love, though that has often a great hand in it. Men of fair minds, and not given up to the overweening of self-flattery, are frequently guilty of it; and in many cases one with amazement hears the arguings, and is astonished at the obstinacy of a worthy man, who yields not to the evidence of reason, though laid before him as clear as daylight.

Not wholly
from Self-love.

(4) I shall be pardoned for calling it [this sort of un-reasonableness] by so harsh a name as madness, when it is considered that opposition to reason deserves that name, and is really madness; and there is scarce a man so free from it, but that if he should always, on all occasions, argue or do as in some cases he constantly does, would not be thought fitter for Bedlam than civil conversation. I do not here mean when he is under the power of an unruly passion, but in the steady calm course of his life. . . .

A Degree of
Madness found
in most Men.

(5) Some of our ideas have a *natural* correspondence and connexion one with another: it is the office and excellency of our reason to trace these, and hold them together in that union and correspondence which is founded in their peculiar beings. Besides this, there is another connexion of ideas wholly owing to *chance* or *custom*. Ideas that in themselves are not all of kin, come to be so united in some men's minds, that it is very hard to separate them; they always keep in company, and the one no sooner at any time comes into the understanding, but its associate appears with it; and if they are more than two which are thus united, the whole gang, always inseparable, show themselves together.

From a wrong
Connexion of
Ideas.

(6) This strong combination of ideas, not allied by nature, the mind makes in itself either voluntarily or by chance; and hence it comes in different men to be very different, according to their different inclina-

This Connexion
made by
custom.

tions, education, interests, &c. *Custom* settles habits of thinking in the understanding, as well as of determining in the will, and of motions in the body: all which seems to be but trains of motions in the animal spirits, which, once set a going, continue in the same steps they have been used to; which, by often treading, are worn into a smooth path, and the motion in it becomes easy, and as it were natural. . . .

(7) That there are such associations of them made by custom, in the minds of most men, I think nobody will question, who has well considered himself or others; and to this, perhaps, might be justly attributed most of the sympathies and antipathies observable in men, which work as strongly, and produce as regular effects as if they were natural; and are therefore called so, though they at first had no other original but the accidental connexion of two ideas, which either the strength of the first impression, or future indulgence so united, that they always afterwards kept company together in that man's mind, as if they were but one idea. . . .

Some Antipathies an Effect of it.

(9) This wrong connexion in our minds of ideas in themselves loose and independent of one another, has such an influence, and is of so great force to set us awry in our actions, as well moral as natural, passions, reasonings, and notions themselves, that perhaps there is not any one thing that deserves more to be looked after.

Wrong connexion of ideas a great Cause of Errors.

(10) The ideas of goblins and sprites have really no more to do with darkness than light: yet let but a foolish maid inculcate these often on the mind of a child, and raise them there together, possibly he shall never be able to separate them again so long as he lives, but darkness shall ever afterwards bring with it those frightful ideas, and they shall be so joined, that he can no more bear the one than the other.

An instance.

(11) A man receives a sensible injury from another, thinks on the man and that action over and over, and by ruminating on them strongly, or much, in his mind, so cements those two ideas together, that he makes them almost one; never thinks on the man, but the pain and displeasure he suffered comes into his mind with it, so that he scarce distinguishes them, but has

Another instance.

as much an aversion for the one as the other. Thus hatreds are often begotten from slight and innocent occasions, and quarrels propagated and continued in the world.

(12) A man has suffered pain or sickness in any place; he saw his friend die in such a room: though these have in nature nothing to do one with another, yet when the idea of the place occurs to his mind, it brings (the impression being once made) that of the pain and displeasure with it: he confounds them in his mind, and can as little bear the one as the other.

A third instance.

(15) Many children, imputing the pain they endured at school to their books they were corrected for, so join those ideas together, that a book becomes their aversion, and they are never reconciled to the study and use of them all their lives after; and thus reading becomes a torment to them, which otherwise possibly they might have made the great pleasure of their lives. There are rooms convenient enough, that some men cannot study in, and fashions of vessels, which, though ever so clean and commodious, they cannot drink out of, and that by reason of some accidential ideas which are annexed to them, and make them offensive; and who is there that hath not observed some man to flag at the appearance, or in the company of some certain person not otherwise superior to him, but because, having once on some occasion got the ascendant, the idea of authority and distance goes along with that of the person, and he that has been thus subjected, is not able to separate them.

More instances.

(16) Instances of this kind are so plentiful everywhere, that if I add one more, it is only for the pleasant oddness of it. It is of a young gentleman, who, having learnt to dance, and that to great perfection, there happened to stand an old trunk in the room where he learnt. The idea of this remarkable piece of household stuff had so mixed itself with the turns and steps of all his dances, that though in that chamber he could dance excellently well, yet it was only whilst that trunk was there; nor could he perform well in any other place, unless that or some such other trunk had its due position in the room. . . .

A curious instance.

The Association of Ideas in Tristram Shandy

The presence in *Tristram Shandy* of what John Locke called the association of ideas has been widely discussed but never completely defined.[1] So it might be well to state here which of the novel's ideas need to be explained as being joined by association and which do not.

Locke, whose *Essay concerning Human Understanding* Sterne quoted as his authority on this subject (8-9), has suggested two ways for recognizing and testing associational connections. First, associational connections are private, personal, different in different men; whenever any man is guilty of an association of ideas, society will call him odd, extravagant, or even mad. Second, associational connections, resulting as they do from chance or custom, do not reflect nature. The first of these criteria was Locke's introduction to the subject of association, the second his formal definition. Since he was not primarily interested in the subject of association, Locke has not bothered to examine these two criteria of his closely; but it is clear that for him the two covered much the same ground: private associations, associations which society in general would reject as odd or extravagant, must surely be unnatural. Sterne, with his vivid sense of social hypocrisy and his great fascination with it, could not agree. Society, as he recognized, rejects, nay, condemns many ideological associations which reflect natural relationships. However, in *Tristram Shandy* he has extensively accounted for both kinds of associations, those that are really unnatural and those whose truth to nature hypocritical society merely refuses to recognize.

The actually unnatural associations reside inside Tristram Shandy's discourse, in the minds of his characters, chiefly in the minds of Walter and Toby Shandy. Their associational predilections, which Tristram has described as their hobbyhorses, lead to the humorous conversational cross purposes which commonly prevail at Shandy Hall.[2] Tristram, of course, never succumbs to any of these associations; indeed, he never presents one of them without making sure his audience can recognize and understand it. His explanations of Shandy associations are often sufficiently pointed to stand with the instances in Locke's *Essay*. One might take as an example Tristram's explanation of his mother's association of clock-winding with sexual intercourse (8-9) or, for its greater economy, his explanation of his father's association of the word "coach" with thoughts of Shandy illegitimacy:

[1] See Arthur H. Cash, "The Lockean Psychology of *Tristram Shandy*," *ELH*, XXII (1955), 70-88, on which discussion I have drawn in writing this note.
[2] See the "Introduction" to Work's edition of the novel, pp. l-li.

Notes and References

. . . at the time my mother's arms were added to the *Shandy's,* when the coach was repainted upon my father's marriage, it had so fallen out, that the coach-painter, whether by performing all his works with the left-hand, like *Turpilius* the *Roman,* or *Hans Holbein* of *Basil*—or whether 'twas more from the blunder of his head than hand—or whether, lastly, it was from the sinister turn, which every thing relating to our family was apt to take—It so fell out, however, to our reproach, that instead of the *bend-dexter,* which since *Harry* the Eighth's reign was honestly our due—a *bend-sinister,* by some of these fatalities, had been drawn quite across the field of the *Shandy-* arms. 'Tis scarce credible that the mind of so wise a man as my father was, could be so much incommoded with so small a matter. The word coach—let it be whose it would—or coach-man, or coach-horse, or coach-hire, could never be named in the family, but he constantly complained of carrying this vile mark of Illegitimacy upon the door of his own; he never once was able to step into the coach, or out of it, without turning round to take a view of the arms, and making a vow at the same time, that it was the last time he would ever set his foot in it again, till the *bend-sinister* was taken out— (313-14)

Tristram has seen perfectly that these unnatural Shandy associations[3] must be explained, must be made publicly viable, if they are to stand in his public discourse. It is, indeed, largely by rehearsing the odd chances and customs which explain them that he has been able to fit into the little room of a few brief moments of Shandy presence the infinite riches of Shandy life.

We may now turn *from* the realm of unnatural associations in *Tristram Shandy.* Before turning *to* the realm of private but natural associations, however, we must remember that Tristram's discourse with society does not depend on either of these kinds of association. All the ideas that Tristram shares with what he calls the world hang together in one or another of those objectively explicable ways that govern all public discourse.[4] These ideas follow one another, from the first idea to the last, in variously chronological and rhetorical ways to form a lucid texture of narrative and argument. All their connections, including those that govern the interruptions of Tristram's audience, would satisfy Locke as not only naturally but publicly explicable.

Some of these connections, it is true, are accompanied and reinforced by what we may call associational grace notes. After his digression on cursing, for example, Tristram resumes his story by recording Susannah's feminine curse, "—Bless my Soul!" (183-4). One need not notice this cursing-curse linkage since the resumption of the story at

[3] For the sake of completeness, I might point out that Mrs. Shandy's association of clock-winding with sexual intercourse, which Tristram (following Locke) labels unnatural (8-9), does nevertheless reflect what Sterne undoubtedly recognized to be a physical resemblance.

[4] See Cash, pp. 127-28, on this point.

this point has been explicitly prepared for (179); but this subliminal chime will no doubt charm the few who catch it. Another such grace note is the wife-wife echo which accompanies Tristram's shift from his interlude on sleep, which was prompted by his story's having reached the time of sleep on his birthday, to the events of the next morning (291). Tristram is concluding this interlude, in the quotation below, by quoting Montaigne on sleep:

I love to lie hard and alone, and even without my wife— This last word may stagger the faith of the world—but remember, "La Vraisemblance (as *Baylet* says in the affair of *Liceti*) n'est pas toujours du Côté de la Verité." And so much for sleep.

CHAP. XVI.

If my wife will but venture him—brother *Toby, Trismegistus* shall be dress'd and brought down to us, whilst you and I are getting our breakfasts together. —(291)

Still another associational grace note is the pere-father link which may be thought to reinforce Tristram's shift from his digression on pre-birth baptism, an element in the introduction of his birthday, to the birthday itself (62-63).

The reader who recognizes these incidental refinements may be led to make some interesting inferences about the material they are embedded in. He may decide, for example, that Susannah's curse overturns the chief assertion of Tristram's digression—that no one can curse outside of Ernulphus's tremendous curse. He may imagine on seeing the wife-wife echo, again, that Walter might often have been inclined, like Montaigne, to lie away from his wife or, on the other hand, to regret that he had ever done so. But the reader need not recognize these grace notes or their implications to follow Tristram's discourse and to derive its essential meanings. They are minor refinements which only appear now and then and which never substitute for the reasonable, public connections of ideas which every ordinarily attentive reader will understand.

Tristram has, then, kept his public discourse publicly connected. But he has not done so without facing a number of temptations to follow private associations. In the digressive interlude on sleep, for instance, Tristram raises the tempting topic of button holes:

It [sleep] is a fine subject!
And yet, as fine as it is, I would undertake to write a dozen chapters upon button-holes, both quicker and with more fame than a single chapter upon this.

Button-holes!—there is something lively in the very idea of 'em—and trust me, when I get amongst 'em—You gentry with great beards—look as grave as you will—I'll make merry work with my button-holes—I shall have 'em all to myself—'tis a maiden subject—I shall run foul of no man's wisdom or fine sayings in it.

But for sleep—I know I shall make nothing of it. . . . (289-90)

The raising of the topic is clear enough: it furnishes an explicitly acknowledged contrast to the topic of sleep. However, the associations it tempts Tristram to seem to be private, socially untenable. But his public commitment to the topic of sleep determines Tristram, as the quotation shows; and he postpones the associationally radiant topic of buttonholes until his discourse allows him to make a public explanation or, at least, a public rationalization for its introduction (363).

Once Tristram does seem to have indulged himself, in public, with a private association:

I have a thing to name—a thing to lament—a thing to hope—a thing to promise, and a thing to threaten—I have a thing to suppose—a thing to declare—a thing to conceal—a thing to chuse, and a thing to pray for.— This chapter, therefore, I *name* the chapter of THINGS—and my next chapter to it, that is, the first chapter of my next volume, if I live, shall be my chapter upon WHISKERS, in order to keep up some sort of connection in my works.

The thing I lament is, that things have crowded in so thick upon me, that I have not been able to get into that part of my work, towards which, I have all the way, looked forwards, with so much earnest desire; and that is the campaigns, but especially the amours of my uncle *Toby*. . . . (336-37)

However, the public requirements of his discourse have even here governed Sterne's narrator. He does not take up the subject of whiskers in the midst of this chapter on things nor even in this volume—so well has he subordinated the private promptings of his mind to his public designs. What *our* minds may lead *us* to may be questionable, but Tristram goes on with things which, as he has informed his audience, this chapter is about. When he does introduce whiskers at the start of the next volume, moreover, his explanation for doing so is not his irresistible private urge but his overwhelming sense of public responsibility:

Upon Whiskers.

I'm sorry I made it—'twas as inconsiderate a promise as ever entered a man's head—A chapter upon whiskers! alas! the world will not bear it—'tis a delicate world—but I knew not of what mettle it was made—nor had I ever seen the underwritten fragment; otherwise, as surely as noses are noses, and whiskers are whiskers still; (let the world say what it will to the contrary) so surely would I have steered clear of this dangerous chapter. (343-44)

He would rather not publicize this associationally explosive material, but a promise is a promise. Tristram will make essentially the same claim, that he has "a small account to settle with the reader," on re-introducing the subject of buttonholes (363).

Tristram's handling of these two subjects exemplifies the realm of private, socially unrecognized association in the novel; and that realm is, of course, the problematical intelligence of Tristram's audience. Sterne has given his social narrator, first, a life whose essential facts are highly provocative of those natural but private associations which society condemns and, second, a highly sensitive social consciousness. It is by the endlessly various manipulation of these two elements of his art that he has been able to invade that so closely guarded realm, the private awareness of social beings. His actual associational creation, however, is merely a vast system of opportunities, a penumbra whose radiance and extent depend on the secret responses of his audience's individual members. We can say little more to define it than that it seems to have cast a more lurid glare in nineteenth-century minds than in any others. But it must be finally a different thing in every different mind. One auditor may be perfectly willing to imagine a breathing organ every time Tristram discusses his "nose," that is, to en-tertain no private associations, no sallies of his imagination; another, say Thackeray, will leap to some private, socially inadmissable notion —a notion he may try to blame on Tristram. The same reader, at one time, may take Tristram's uses of "crevice," "channel," and "centre" quite vaguely and simply and, at another, leap from them to precise and indecent ideas. One reader, again, may read about Bobby Shan-dy's projected ingress, egress, and regress into foreign parts and about the *a posteriori* road to preferment with a clear mind but find that Corporal Trim's freely waving stick, that symbol of celibacy, power-fully awakens a private association.

Tristram's own associations are, of course, problematical. None of his many warnings, such as this one to my dear girl, allows us to go beyond the thoughts he allows himself to share with us: "Now don't let Satan, my dear girl, in this chapter, take advantage of any one spot of rising-ground to get astride of your imagination, if you can any ways help it; or if he is so nimble as to slip on,—let me beg of you, like an unback'd filly, *to frisk it, to squirt it, to jump it, to rear it, to bound it,—and to kick it, with long kicks and short kicks,* till like *Tickletoby's* mare, you break a strap or a crupper, and throw his worship into the dirt.—You need not kill him—" (226). We cannot even be sure in Tristram's few moments of apparent mental disarray exactly what is in his mind. "—Fair and softly, gentle reader!—where is thy fancy carrying thee?—

If there is truth in man, by my great grandfather's nose, I mean the external organ of smelling, or that part of man which stands prominent in his face,—and which painters say, in good jolly noses and well-proportioned faces, should comprehend a full third,—that is, measuring downwards from the setting on of the hair.—[¶]—What a life of it has an author, at this pass!" (221). Not quite sure even here. The point is, of course, that Tristram's associations are not part of the novel: he gets his peculiarly unmentionable life miraculously before us without exposing any of them.

The associational material of *Tristram Shandy*, then, lies, first, inside the discourse in the hobbyhorsical minds of Tristram's characters and, second, outside the discourse in the problematical imaginations of Tristram's audience. The first of these associational realms Tristram has made so clear and plain that no critic of the novel need explain it. The second, which is a mere penumbra (although obviously a powerfully affective one), no critic can explain. It is, of course, Tristram's clear but endlessly provocative discourse which does present rich grounds for critical description.

7. Pringle-Pattison's edition of the *Essay*, esp. p. 109 where Locke says that the train of ideas from which we derive our sense of duration, "varies not very much [in its speed] in a waking man"; or p. 121 where he says that man's "thoughts are but of yesterday, and he knows not what tomorrow will bring forth. What is once past he can never recall; and what is yet to come, he cannot make present."

8. *An Introduction to the English Novel*, I (London, 1951), 82.

Chapter Two

1. All my citations and parenthetical page notations refer to the edition by James Aiken Work (New York, 1960).

2. *The English Humorists of the Eighteenth Century* (New York, 1864), p. 241.

3. In "The self-conscious Narrator in Prose Fiction before *Tristram Shandy*," *PMLA*, LXVII (1952), 181-83.

4. In my article, "Tristram Shandy's Tragicomical Testimony," *Criticism*, III (1961), 171-85.

5. In the "Introduction" to his edition of the novel, pp. lx-lxi.

6. See Wayne C. Booth, "Did Sterne Complete *Tristram Shandy?*" *MP*, XLVIII (1951), 172-83.

7. In "*Tristram Shandy* and the Tradition of Learned Wit," *Essays in Criticism*, I (1951), 239-40.

8. See Booth, "Did Sterne Complete *Tristram Shandy?*" p. 174; also

Letters of Laurence Sterne, ed. Lewis Perry Curtis (Oxford, 1935), pp. 284;288;294.

9. See Coleridge's fine remarks on Sterne's feeling for the "minutiae" of life, *Complete Works,* IV (New York, 1871), 281-85.

10. See Ben Reid, "The Sad Hilarity of Sterne," *VQR,* XXXII (1956), 107-30 for a general statement of Sterne's tragic sense of life.

11. *English Humorists,* p. 246.

12. *Literary Studies,* II (London, 1910), 301.

13. It should be noted here in general how the three aspects of the social unsuitableness of Tristram's material interact in his discourse: he has variously eased the public expression of his life's oddity by playing on its tragedy and obscenity, and eased its tragedy by playing on its oddity and obscenity, and eased its obscenity by playing on its oddity and tragedy. The reader will notice many incidental recognitions of this interaction in the following chapters; actually, there are few passages in the novel in which these three aspects of Tristram's discursive problem, which I have isolated for the purposes of analysis, do not mesh in one way or another.

Chapter Three

1. See *Complete Works,* IV (New York, 1871), 275-85 for all the material referred to in this paragraph.

2. See, for instance, Alan B. Howes, *Yorick and The Critics* (New Haven, 1958), pp. 35-37 and Arthur Cash, "The Lockean Psychology of *Tristram Shandy,*" *ELH,* XII (1955), 131 for fairly representative explanations of the digressions.

3. Here is a fuller analysis of Tristram's Preface for those who may need or desire it.

Tristram's Preface on the distribution of wit and judgment (192-203) is composed of a main point and a subordinate point. The subordinate point, which Tristram argues first, asserts the lack of a plenitude of wit and judgment. It is divided into three parts: the first and third argue logically, the second by a climate analogy. The first and third parts argue that we would act in certain ways if we had plenty of wit and judgment, that we do not act in these ways, and, therefore, that we do not have plenty. The first part, which tells how sharply we would all attack one another with our plenitude of wit and then how graciously we would smooth things over with our plenitude of judgment, seems largely fanciful at first. Tristram has called it "the first insinuating *How d'ye* of a caressing prefacer." The third part, which describes how odd the conduct of different professions would be if their practitioners had a plenitude of wit and judgment, is admittedly satirical. The second part of this section describes a tour from the icy wastes of Lapland and Nova Zembla, where there is the least wit and judgment and the least need of them, to the erratic climate of England with its erratic outbursts and absences of wit and judgment. The lack of general plenitude, argued by all three parts, is explicitly stated between the first and second parts and again between the second and third.

Having made this subordinate point, Tristram formally turns to "the main and principal point I have taken to clear up." It is: "How it comes to pass, that your men of least *wit* are reported to be men of most *judgment*." His attack on this report has two parts. In the first, Tristram argues that the report is false by establishing that there is a balance of wit and judgment in every man. He does this by referring to the two knobs of his chair; but he is actually arguing from his unstated certainty in God's wisdom and orderliness. In the second part, he explains how the false report of inbalances in the distribution of wit and judgment, whose falsity he has just shown, got started.

Tristram has asserted a strong connection between the two points of his Preface: "by the help of the observations already premised [in making the subordinate point], and I hope already weighed and perpended by your reverences and worships," he says, "I shall forthwith make [the main point] appear." This help is not a logically necessary one. For, although we must be certain of a lack of wit and judgment to argue their distribution, the mere lack does not certify the distribution Tristram is arguing for any more than it does the distribution he opposes. We can, however, see a strong conversational *ad hominem* help for the main point in Tristram's conduct of the subordinate one. His easy joining of wit and judgment in the second and third parts of the subordinate section would accustom Tristram's audience to think of them together and thus to think of them as going together. The second part, which makes both equally dependent on climate, would be especially effective in asserting their proper union. This sub-rational joining of the two, before rationally arguing for their joining, would be strengthened by the first part of the subordinate section which has, by separating wit and judgment, made a joke out of perfect wittiness with no judgment to restrain it and perfect restraint with nothing to restrain. Even more important, perhaps, is the strong assertion of a wise God, who gives us all the wit and judgment we need, with which Tristram concludes his verbal tour from Lapland to England. It makes Tristram's dependence on a wise God in his crucial argument for the balance of wit and judgment in every man seem natural and right.

The relationship between these two sections of the Preface is, then, not a logical one. Nor is any part of the Preface philosophically binding, not even the key argument. An argument based on the wisdom of a creator, when neither his wisdom nor even his existence has been established, has no philosophical validity. It is thus an error to speak of this Preface of Tristram's as a corrective to Locke. Tristram is here in a public argument with Your Reverences and Worships, with men, we may say, who profess belief in a wise and orderly creator and yet defend the odd distribution of wit and judgment which, of course, allows them to claim the latter. As an effort to laugh and argue away their continued holding to the odd distribution (if, as Tristram does not insist, they now hold to it) and as a revelation to the rest of society of their absurdity in holding to it, the Preface is wonderfully trenchant and effective. And that, of course, is its purpose in Tristram's discourse.

4. The Modern Library edition (New York, 1950) which is the source of my quotations and to which my parenthetical pagination refers.

5. Wayne C. Booth, "The Self-conscious Narrator in Prose Fiction before *Tristram Shandy*," *PMLA*, LXVII (1952), 175-80.

Chapter Four

1. *Perilous Balance* (Princeton, 1939), pp. 103ff.

2. "Did Sterne Complete *Tristram Shandy?*" *MP*, XLVIII (1951), 172-83.

3. *Aspects of the Novel* (New York, 1927), pp. 157-80.

4. The Modern Library edition (New York, 1950) which is the (1936), 803-20.

5. In this connection see an excellent article by William J. Farrell, "Nature Versus Art as a Comic Pattern in *Tristram Shandy*," *ELH*, XXX (1963), esp. 29-35.

6. *Tristram Shandy's World* (Berkeley, 1954), pp. 42;43.

7. *The English Novel* (New York, 1953), p. 83.

8. "Of Time, Personality and the Author," *Studies in the Comic, University of California Publications in English,* VIII, iv (1941), 240.

9. *Perilous Balance,* p. 153.

10. "The Lockean Psychology of *Tristram Shandy*," *ELH*, XXII (1955), 133.

11. *Diderot and Sterne* (New York, 1955), p. 145.

12. "The Reinterpretation of Laurence Sterne," *Etudes Anglaise,* VII (1954), 44; and a rev. of *Tristram Shandy's World* in SR, LXIII (1955), 689.

Chapter Five

1. See, for instance, Sigurd Burkhardt, *"Tristram Shandy's* Law of Gravity," *ELH*, XXVIII (1961), esp. 72-75.

2. See Spectator No. 63 in *The Spectator*, Everyman's Library, I (New York, 1930), esp. 232-33.

3. See, for instance, Thackeray's *English Humorists of the Eighteenth Century* (London, 1912), pp. 228-71 and Bagehot's *Literary Studies*, II (London, 1910), 94-130.

4. Work's edition has "defended" instead of "defeated" in the last line of this quotation; but this seems to disagree with all other editions of *Tristram Shandy*, including the first one.

Chapter Six

1. *Letters of Laurence Sterne*, ed. Lewis Perry Curtis (Oxford, 1935), p. 411.

Chapter Seven

1. I have derived the statement on Sterne's life in this and the next paragraphs largely from Wilbur Cross, *The Life and Times of Laurence Sterne* (New Haven, 1929), pp. 93-225.

2. *Ibid.*, p. 102; these are Sterne's own words in a letter to his uncle.

3. *Ibid.*, p. 111.

4. D. W. Jefferson, *Laurence Sterne* (London, 1954), p. 14.

Chapter Eight

1. Ed. L. A. Selby-Bigge (Oxford, 1951), p. xx.

2. Rambler No. 4, reprinted in *The Works of Samuel Johnson*, I (New York, 1903), 20-21; all my Johnson citations refer to this edition.

3. *The History of Rasselas, Prince of Abissinia, Works*, VII.

4. For a more extensive discussion of Johnson's empiricism see Jean Hagstrum, *Samuel Johnson's Literary Criticism* (Minneapolis, 1952), pp. 3-20.

5. *Treatise*, pp. xxii-xxiii.

6. All my *A Sentimental Journey* citations refer to the edition by Wilbur Cross (New York, 1926).

7. See esp. Chapt. 3, Sect. III of this book.

8. *Letters of Laurence Sterne*, ed. Lewis Perry Curtis (Oxford, 1935), p. 401.

9. Alice Green Fredman's expression in her *Diderot and Sterne* (New York, 1955), pp. 194-95.

10. "Philanthropy Recommended," in *The Writings of Laurence Sterne*, VI (Boston, 1927), 26.

11. "Follow Peace," in *Writings,* VII, 217.

12. "Vindication of Human Nature," in *Writings,* VI, 83.

13. *Sterne* (London, 1910), pp. 14; 149.

14. *Letters,* pp. 401-02 where Sterne talks of love as a tide that can be variously directed.

15. *Letters,* p. 256.

16. *London Journal,* ed. Frederick A. Pottle (New York, 1950), pp. 127-28.

Chapter Nine

1. "The Evolution of *A Sentimental Journey*," *PQ,* XIX (1940), 368.

2. *The Unsentimental Journey of Laurence Sterne* (New York, 1948), p. 98.

3. *Ibid.,* p. 60.

4. "Laurence Sterne, Apostle of Laughter," *The Age of Johnson,* pres. to C.B. Tinker (New Haven, 1949), p. 169.

5. In his "Introduction" to *A Sentimental Journey* (London, 1929), pp. xxxii-xxxiv.

6. *A Tale of a Tub with other Early Works,* ed. Herbert Davis (Oxford, 1957), esp. pp. 84-89.

7. Reprinted in *The Best of Pope,* ed. George Sherburn (New York, 1940), p. 127.

8. *Treatise,* pp. 187-219.

9. *Works,* VII, 94.

Selected Bibliography

One can broaden, but by no means complete, this brief list of Sterne material by reference to the Cambridge *Bibliography of English Literature*, 4 vols. (Cambridge: The University Press, 1941) and its *Supplement*, vol. V (Cambridge: The University Press, 1957), to *English Literature 1660-1800*, 4 vols. (Princeton: Princeton University Press, 1950 ff) and its yearly continuation in the July Number of *PQ*, and to *Laurence Sterne, a List of Critical Studies* (Brooklyn: Long Island University Press, 1948).

PRIMARY SOURCES

STERNE, LAURENCE. *Letters of Laurence Sterne*. Ed. Lewis Perry Curtis. Oxford: The Clarendon Press, 1935.

————. *The Life and Opinions of Tristram Shandy, Gentleman*. Ed. James A. Work. New York: The Odyssey Press, 1940. This is an indispensable document for the student of Sterne for its introduction, its notes, and its text. One should note, however, one significant textual error—"defended" instead of the correct "defeated" on p. 626.

————. *The Life and Works of Laurence Sterne*. 12 vols. Ed. Wilbur Cross. New York: J. F. Taylor, 1904.

————. *A Political Romance*. Ed. Wilbur Cross. Boston: The Club of Odd Volumes, 1914.

————. *A Sentimental Journey Through France and Italy with Selections from the Journals, Sermons, and Correspondence*. Ed. Wilbur Cross. New York: Boni and Liveright, 1926.

————. *A Sentimental Journey through France and Italy*. New York: Everyman's Library, 1960.

————. *A Sentimental Journey Through France and Italy*. New York: Macdonald, 1950. This and the Everyman's edition of *Journey* are handier than the Cross edition; but their punctuation has been arbitrarily "regularized."

————. *The Writings of Laurence Sterne.* 7 vols. Boston: Houghton, Mifflin, 1926-27.

SECONDARY SOURCES

1. *Chiefly on Sterne's Life*

CROSS, WILBUR. *The Life and Times of Laurence Sterne.* New Haven: Yale University Press, 1929. This is the authoritative life.

CURTIS, L. P. *The Politics of Laurence Sterne.* Oxford: Oxford University Press, 1929. This book fills in the biography, describing Sterne's political activities in York in the early 1740's.

ELWIN, WHITWELL. *Some Eighteenth Century Men of Letters.* 2 vols. London: J. Murray, 1902. Contains (II, 1-81) good studies of the Shandys—as part of a brief biography of Sterne.

HARTLEY, LODWICK. *This is Lorence.* Chapel Hill: University of North Carolina Press, 1943. A graceful, entertaining recounting of Sterne's life and career.

QUENNELL, PETER. "Laurence Sterne," in *The Profane Virtues.* New York: Viking Press, 1945. A brief life.

SHAW, M. R. B. *Laurence Sterne: The Making of a Humorist, 1713-1762.* London: Richards Press, 1957. This book helps especially to fill in the intellectual and literary sides of Sterne's career.

SICHEL, WALTER. *Sterne.* London: Williams and Norgate, 1910. An impressionistic study of Sterne's life whose opening remarks are very illuminating.

TRAILL, H. D. *Sterne.* New York: Harper, 1887. Chiefly a biography, but containing two critical chapters, one on Sterne's humor and sentiment and one on his dramatic power, which are still valuable.

2. *Chiefly on Sterne's Writings.*

BAGEHOT, WALTER. *Literary Studies.* 2 vols. London: J. M. Dent, 1910. Contains an essay on "Sterne and Thackeray" (II, 94-130) which, despite some typical Victorian biases, makes some valuable comments on Sterne's style.

BAIRD, THEODORE. "The Time-scheme of *Tristram Shandy* and a source," *PMLA*, LI (1936), 803-20. A valuable demonstration of the novel's chronological exactitude.

BAKER, ERNEST A. *The History of the English Novel.* 10 vols. London: H. F. and G. Witherby, 1924-39. Contains an essay on "Sterne" (IV, 240-77) which sets his work in the stream of English fiction.

BIRKHEAD, EDITH. "Sentiment and Sensibility in the Eighteenth Century Novel," *Essays and Studies,* XI (1925), 92-116. Gives useful background to a study of sentiment in Sterne.

BOOTH, WAYNE C. "Did Sterne Complete *Tristram Shandy?*" *MP,* XLVIII (1951), 172-83. This article, drawn from Booth's doctoral thesis (Chicago, 1950), argues convincingly that he did.

————. *The Rhetoric of Fiction.* Chicago: University of Chicago Press, 1962. Booth has described *Tristram* (pp. 221-40) as an exemplification of his thesis that fiction is, among other things, a design upon its readers.

————. "The Self-conscious Narrator in Prose Fiction before *Tristram Shandy,*" *PMLA,* LXVII (1952), 163-85. This article, also drawn from Booth's doctoral thesis, works towards a definition of the novel's basic form by describing its fictional precursors.

BOYS, RICHARD C. "*Tristram Shandy* and the conventional Novel," *Papers of the Michigan Academy of Science, Arts and Letters,* XXXVII (1951), 423-36. Chiefly useful as a survey of *Tristram* criticism from the time of Sterne to that of Joyce.

BURCKHARDT, SIGURD. "*Tristram Shandy's* Law of Gravity," *ELH,* XXVIII (1961), 70-88. A highly personal but provocative discussion of the novel.

CASH, ARTHUR H. "The Lockean Psychology of *Tristram Shandy,*" *ELH,* XXII (1955), 125-35. Completely explodes the old notion that Tristram yoked his ideas together through "association."

COLERIDGE, SAMUEL TAYLOR. *Complete Works.* 7 vols. New York: Harper, 1871. Contains a few fine comments on Sterne (IV, 275-85), especially on his handling of the "minutiae of thought" and on the "humanistic universality" of each separate part of *Tristram.*

DILWORTH, ERNEST. *The Unsentimental Journey of Laurence Sterne.* New York: King's Crown Press, 1948. Flippant insistence on the flippant (especially as opposed to the sentimental) intentions of Sterne.

ELTON, OLIVER. *A Survey of English Literature 1830-1870.* 2 vols. New York: Macmillan, 1928. A brief account (I, 217-31) of Sterne's career and writings.

FARRELL, WILLIAM J. "Nature Versus Art as a Comic Pattern in *Tristram Shandy,*" *ELH,* XXX (1963), 16-35. An excellent article.

FERRIAR, JOHN. *Illustrations of Sterne.* London: Cadell and Davies, 1912. Ferriar, almost the first serious student of Sterne, showed chiefly the extent of the novelist's borrowings.

FLUCHÈRE, HENRI. *Laurence Sterne etc.* Paris: Gallimard, 1961. A biography of Sterne and an extensive discussion of elements of his style (technique, structure, themes etc.).

FORSTER, E. M. *Aspects of the Novel.* New York: Harcourt, Brace, 1927. Forster makes an interesting statement on *Tristram* (pp. 157-80).

FOSTER, JAMES R. *The History of the Pre-Romantic Novel in England.* New York: Modern Language Assn., 1949. Places Sterne generally in the stream of sentiment and sensibility (especially pp. 130-38).

FREDMAN, ALICE GREEN. *Diderot and Sterne.* New York: Columbia University Press, 1955. A valuable study although the focus on Sterne has been sometimes blurred for the sake of the comparison.

HAMMOND, LANSING VAN DER HEYDEN. *Sterne's Sermons of Mr. Yorick.* New Haven: Yale University Press, 1948. This indispensable guide to a study of the sermons shows Sterne's borrowings and his originality.

HOWES, ALAN B. *Yorick and the Critics: Sterne's Reputation in England, 1760-1868.* New Haven: Yale University Press, 1958. A clear and comprehensive description of Sterne's critical ups and downs —a valuable book.

JEFFERSON, D. W. *Laurence Sterne.* London: Longmans, Green, 1954. A handy, compact introduction to Sterne and his writings.

————. "*Tristram Shandy* and the Tradition of Learned Wit," *Essays in Criticism,* I (1951), 225-48. A trenchant account of Sterne's use and his satire of learning.

KETTLE, ARNOLD. *An Introduction to the English Novel.* 2 vols. London: Hutchinson's University Library, 1951. An excellent account of *Tristram* (I, 81-87), especially in its description of the tension in the novel between human pretensions and "the cussedness of life."

LEHMAN, B. H. "Of Time, Personality and the Author," *Studies in the Comic, University of California Publications in English,* VIII, iv (1941), 233-50. A seminal statement of the notion that *Tristram's* unity is that of Tristram's consciousness. Fluchère, for instance, has praised this article (pp. 303-04; 474-76) and built on it.

MCKILLOP, ALAN D. *Early Masters of the English Novel.* Lawrence: University of Kansas Press, 1956. In his chapter on Sterne (V, 182-219), McKillop gives an eloquent and perceptive discussion of the novels.

MACLEAN, KENNETH. *John Locke and English Literature of the Eighteenth Century.* New Haven: Yale University Press, 1936. Valuable background to Sterne; MacLean argues that Sterne is almost always (except in his account of wit and judgment) in line with Locke's philosophy.

MUIR, EDWIN. *Essays in Literature and Society*. London: Hogarth Press, 1949. Contains a beautifully evocative essay on "Laurence Sterne" (pp. 49-56).

PUTNEY, RUFUS. "Laurence Sterne, Apostle of Laughter," in *The Age of Johnson*. New Haven: Yale University Press, 1949. In this packed article (pp. 159-70), Putney stresses the inter-relationships between Sterne's works and his career.

———. "The Evolution of *A Sentimental Journey*," *PQ*, XIX (1940) 349-69. Putney argues cogently that the *Journey* is "a hoax by which Sterne persuaded his contemporaries that the humor he wanted to write was the pathos they wished to read."

READ, HERBERT. *The Sense of Glory*. New York: Harcourt, Brace, 1930. In his essay on "Sterne" (pp. 124-51), Read gives an excellent appreciation of Sterne, especially of his *Journey*.

REID, BEN. "The Sad Hilarity of Sterne," *VQR*, XXXII (1956), 107-30. Points out in general terms the tragicomic complex in Sterne's nature and art.

ROLLE, DIETRICH. *Fielding und Sterne: Untersuchungen über die Funktion des Erzählers*. Münster: Verlag Aschendorff, 1963. I have not yet seen this recent addition to the study of Sterne.

RUSSELL, H. K. "*Tristram Shandy* and the Technique of the Novel," *SP*, XLII (1945), 581-93. A stepping-stone toward our present understanding of *Tristram*: insists on our separating Tristram from Sterne and seeing him as a fictional character.

STEDMOND, J. M. "Genre and *Tristram Shandy*," *PQ*, XXXVIII (1959), 37-51. Stedmond has rationalized a favorite modern way of looking at *Tristram*, that is, as a mental stream and a mental portrait (and thus as a precursor to Joyce) by a discussion of the novel's literary antecedents.

———. "Satire and *Tristram Shandy*," *SEL*, I (1961), 53-63. An excellent but largely undeveloped perception, that *Tristram* was "aimed at the public itself."

———. "Sterne as Plagiarist," *English Studies*, XLI (1960), 308-12. A valuable corrective to the old belief that Sterne was a wholesale plagiarist.

———. "Style and *Tristram Shandy*," *MLQ*, XX (1959), 243-51. A good discussion of rhythmic and verbal elements in Sterne's style and their links with earlier literature.

THACKERAY, WILLIAM MAKEPEACE. *The English Humorists of the Eighteenth Century*. New York: Harper, 1864. Thackeray's attack on Sterne (pp. 228-71) is valuable as an indication—if an extreme one—of nineteenth-century feelings.

TOWERS, A. R. "Sterne's Cock and Bull Story," *ELH*, XXIV (1957), 12-29. A fine discussion of *Tristram,* approaching the novel's problems and qualities by studying its treatment of sex.

TRAUGOTT, JOHN. *Tristram Shandy's World.* Berkeley: University of California Press, 1954. An arguable description of *Tristram* enhanced by many excellent insights.

VAN GHENT, DOROTHY. *The English Novel.* New York: Rinehart, 1953. Professor Van Ghent, following B. H. Lehman (above), focusses "On *Tristram Shandy*" (pp. 83-98 of her book) as a mental portrait and a precursor to Proust and Joyce.

WATKINS, W.B.C. *Perilous Balance.* Princeton: Princeton University Press, 1939. "Yorick Revisited" in this volume (pp. 99-156) is a sensitive interweaving of Sterne criticism and biography done, Watkins explains, because "an understanding of his [Sterne's] personality is peculiarly important to an understanding of his works."

WATT, IAN. *The Rise of the Novel.* Berkeley: University of California Press, 1957. A fine discussion of the English novel as it developed up to Sterne's time, which contains several provocative comments on Sterne (pp. 290-95).

WEALES, GERALD. "Tristram Shandy's Anti-book," in *Twelve Original Essays.* Detroit: Wayne State University Press, 1960. This essay (pp. 43-67 in the book) describes *Tristram* as "Sterne's humorous view of himself and his world."

WOOLF, VIRGINIA. *The Second Common Reader.* New York: Harcourt, Brace, 1932. An essay on the *Journey* (pp. 80-88) which finds that it "is based on something fundamentally philosophic."

Index

Proust, Marcel, 5, 15
Putney, Rufus, 106, 107

Quennell, Peter, 3

Rabelais, François, 3
Rasselas (Johnson), 18, 93, 94
Read, Sir Herbert, 109
Reynolds, Sir Joshua, 88-89

Sentimental Journey, A (Sterne), 91-112; empiricism of, 93-95; form and technique, 95-99; general benevolence, 100; sentiment and candor, 106-7; sentiment and self-love, 105-6; sentimental absurdity, 103-5; sentimentality defined, 99-100; Sterne's method of instruction, 100-102; use of contrast, 96; use of generalization, 96-97; use of relevant material, 95
Sermons (of Sterne), 10, 13, 134
Shaw, Margaret R. B., 3
Sichel, Walter, 100
Smollett, Tobias, 113
Sterne, Jacques (Sterne's uncle), 10, 88
Sterne, Laurence, chronology of life, 9-11; fame, 89; in York politics, 88; jailing of mother, 88; London social triumphs, 88-90; retreat to country parish, 88; success of *Tristram Shandy*, 88; view of society, 88; (for works by Sterne see *Tristram Shandy* and *A Sentimental Journey*)
Sterne, Lydia (Sterne's daughter), 9, 10, 11
Sterne, Roger (Sterne's father), 9
Sterne's Politics (Curtis), 3
Sutherland, James, 16
Swift, Jonathan, 3, 15, 16, 89, 110

Tale of a Tub, A (Swift), 15, 21
Thackeray, William Makepeace, 15, 22, 29
This is Lorence (Hartley), 3
Tom Jones (Fielding), 44, 45, 46
Traugott, John, 62
Treatise of Human Nature (Hume), 93, 94
Tristram Shandy (Sterne), 19-87; chance, equivocation of, 58-60; chance, presentation of, 49-51; choice of words, 69-74; comic tone, maintenance of, 56-64; compared with *Tom Jones*, 44-46; death, equivocation of, 56-58; death, presentation of, 47-49; didactic tone, 66-69; digressions, explanatory, 32-34; digressions, internal forms of, 36-41; digressions, opinionative, 34-35; digressions, use of, 31-46; facts of his life, 25-27; form of presentation, 26-30; his social situation, 21-25; his tragicomical transformation, 47-65; interlude, use of, 35; sex, view of, 79-84; style, 23-24; suggestive names, use of, 72-73; suspensions, use of, 75-79; social unsuitableness of facts, 28-30, 126; time, equivocation of, 60-63; time, presentation of, 51-56; wit, 73

Ulysses (Joyce), 115

Van Ghent, Dorothy, 62

Warburton, William (Bishop of Gloucester), 88
Watkins, W. B. C., 47, 63
Wilkes, John, 16
Woolf, Virginia, 15, 16
Work, James A., 25

DATE DUE